THE IRISH-AMERICANS

THE IRISH-AMERICANS

IRISH NATIONALISM
AND THE AMERICAN CONTRIBUTION

Edited, with an Introduction
by Lawrence J. McCaffrey

ARNO PRESS

A New York Times Company

New York — 1976

Editorial Supervision: ANDREA HICKS

———◆———

Reprint Edition 1976 by Arno Press, Inc.
Copyright © 1976 by Arno Press, Inc.
"Nationalism and the Irish Peasant" and
"The Origins and Character of Irish-American
Nationalism" by Thomas N. Brown were reprinted
by permission of The Review of Politics.

"Irish Nationalism and Irish Catholicism" by
Lawrence J. McCaffrey was reprinted by permission
of Church History.

"America and the Irish Problem, 1899-1921"
by Alan J. Ward was reprinted by permission
of Irish Historical Studies.

THE IRISH-AMERICANS
ISBN for complete set: 0-405-09317-9
See last pages of this volume for titles.

Manufactured in the United States of America

———◆———

Library of Congress Cataloging in Publication Data
Main entry under title:

Irish nationalism and the American contribution.

(The Irish-Americans)
Includes bibliographical references.
CONTENTS: McCaffrey, L. J. The American and
Catholic dimensions of Irish nationalism.--Brown,
T. N. Nationalism and the Irish peasant, 1800-1848.
--McCaffrey, L. J. Irish nationalism and Irish
Catholicism. [etc.]
    1. Irish question--Addresses, essays, lectures.
2. Irish Americans--Addresses, essays, lectures.
3. United States--Foreign relations--Great Britain--
Addresses, essays, lectures. 4. Great Britain--
Foreign relations--United States--Addresses, essays,
lectures. I. McCaffrey, Lawrence John, 1925-
II. Series.
DA950.I7 1976   301.29'415'073   76-6354
ISBN 0-405-09347-0

CONTENTS

INTRODUCTION

Although Irish nationalism has been expressed in some of the finest examples of modern literature, in essence it is a simple creed. Its contents have been borrowed from the common currency of Western thought. Nationalists — constitutional and revolutionary — who have argued for Irish independence from British colonialism have presented their case in the rhetoric of John Locke and British Whiggery as passed on through the medium of eighteenth-century Anglo-Irish Protestant patriotism.[1] The nineteenth-century alliances between Irish constitutional nationalists and the British left — Donald O'Connell with the Radicals and Whigs, Charles Stewart Parnell with the Liberals — plus the American experience of the majority of Irish emigrants strengthened the Irish commitment to the values of liberalism. Physical force nationalists were also in the liberal, popular sovereignty mold, taking their inspiration from the romantic, liberal nationalism of the Continent — Mazzini and Garibaldi — and the republicanism of the United States.[2]

In the 1840s Irish nationalism began to move beyond the political boundaries outlined by O'Connell and, under the tutorship of Young Ireland, embraced a cultural dimension. Its ideological source was the anti-industrial, anti-urban romanticism that influenced intellectual attitudes in all parts of Europe. Young Irelanders and subsequent apostles of Irish cultural nationalism denounced British values as the epitome of urban, industrial materialism threatening the rural, spiritual essence of Irish culture.

One of the ingredients in the gospel of Young Ireland was the preservation and cultivation of the native language as an expression of the Irish soul and as a barrier against the advance of

British culture. In the revival of cultural nationalism in the 1890s, manifested in the Gaelic League, the Gaelic Athletic Association, and the literary renaissance, the role of the Irish language increased in significance. The Irish-Ireland ideal became an important motivating force in the revolutionary thrust that finally liberated three-fourths of Ireland from British rule in December, 1921. The Irish-Ireland goal of the language movement's cultural nationalism was an Irish expression of the "racial" aspect present in European nationalism since the early nineteenth-century when Prussian nationalists used folk, race and blood arguments to energize their people against the imperialism of the French Revolution. Late in the nineteenth-century, Social Darwinism, employed as a justification for European and American imperialisms, intensified the racial quotient in nationalism. Since Anglo-Saxon racism became a major ideological argument for British and American imperialisms and a reason to keep the "inferior" Celtic Irish down in the United Kingdom and the United States, the Irish reacted by cultivating their own brand of racism, hence the popularity of the Irish-Ireland movement.[3]

Although Irish nationalism lacks uniqueness in the contents of its message, it is original in some of its manifestations. Irish nationalism established a close identity with Catholicism, and the Irish were the first Europeans to transport their nationalism and cultivate it in America. In his *Essays on Nationalism* (New York: 1926) and *The Historical Evolution of Modern Nationalism* (New York: 1931), Carleton J. H. Hayes described modern nationalism as a religious heresy, a creed substituting the nation state for the God of the Jews and Christians, a faith that captured the allegiance and the imagination of the Western masses after Christianity failed to satisfy their psychological and emotional needs for certitude, liturgy, and security. Irish nationalism contradicts the Hayes' thesis. It has always been associated with Catholic Christianity, establishing twin religious and ethnic identities.

Irish nationalist apologists and ideologists have always insisted that the associations between Irish and Catholic were accidental rather than essential, emphasizing that the roots of their movement can be traced back to the eighteenth-century conversion of Anglo-Irish Protestants from agents of British colonialism to advocates of an independent Irish nation. And they point out that from the time of O'Connell in the early nineteenth-century to the present day, Irish nationalists have rejected Catholic power, inviting Protestants to join them in creating a united, non-sectarian nation state. These invitations have been sincere. Irish nationalists have continually exalted the Anglo-Irish Protestant contribution to Irish politics and culture, and when they finally created a twenty-six county Irish nation state, they wrote liberal-democratic constitutions guaranteeing equality and civil rights to the small Protestant minority whose sixteenth, seventeenth, and eighteenth-centuries ancestors served as the British colony in Ireland, conquering and enslaving the Catholic majority.[4]

From the beginning the ecumenism of Irish nationalism was more myth than reality because the vast majority of Irish Protestants wanted no part of a liberal-democratic, non-sectarian Irish nation. Almost all of the leaders of eighteenth-century Anglo-Irish Protestant patriotism insisted that the liberties that they extorted from a Britain losing a war to American revolutionaries and their French and Spanish allies applied only to the Protestant minority. They refused Catholics basic civil rights.[5] During the Union period (1801-1921), Protestant Ireland, with only a few exceptions, rejected nationalist offers to join freedom movements such as Repeal and Home Rule, Protestants fervently declared their loyalty to the British connection as a shield protecting Protestant life, property and Ascendancy from the power lusts of a Catholic democracy stimulated by "the agents of Vatican intrigue and ambition." Militant Ulster Protestant opposition to Home Rule and Republicanism, endorsed by British no-popery, resulted in the partition of Ireland. Like its eighteenth-century Anglo-Irish Protestant model, Northern Ireland emerged as a "Protestant nation for a Protestant people," condemning a large Catholic minority to ghettos of poverty and paranoia.

Oh, Irish nationalism garnered some ideas and values from the Anglo-Irish Protestant experience — Whig political theories and institutions and the precedent and tradition of a largely autonomous Irish nation — but the essence of the Irish identity was Catholicism. In the sixteenth and seventeenth-centuries the English employed Protestantism as their crusading cause to justify the conquest and plantation of Ireland as a way of securing Britain from the menaces of Catholic Spain and France. This Protestant strategy forced the Irish to embrace Catholicism as a symbol of their separate cultural identity. After the English conquerors subdued the clan chiefs, Catholicism replaced an aristocratic Gaelic culture as the identity symbol of the peasant masses who were reduced to the humbling and humiliating condition of serfdom. In the late seventeenth and early eighteenth-centuries, following the total military defeat of Catholic Ireland, the Irish Protestant Parliament enacted Penal Laws designed to humiliate and demoralize the Catholic majority, rendering them incapable of successful rebellion. The refusal of the late eighteenth-century Protestant nation to lift the burdens of apartheid from the Catholic people; the loyalty of nineteenth and twentieth-centuries Irish Protestants to the Union and British identity; and Anglo-Saxon Protestant, anti-Irish, no-popery nativism in both the United Kingdom and the United States combined to cement the ties between Irish and Catholic.[6]

Anti-Catholicism in Britain and America was one link that united the Irish of the diaspora to those who remained home, forcing them to retain their ethnicity and encouraging them to contribute their energy, enthusiasm, and dollars to the cause of Irish nationalism. In his *States of Ireland* (New York: 1972), Conor Cruise O'Brien observes that "The beginnings of the Irish revolution — that is, the revolution of the Catholic Irish — are as much in America as in Ireland." That is an understatement: the nationalism and the revolution of the Catholic Irish was more in America than Ireland. Irish-Americans hated Britain and things British with an intensity and passion far beyond what was felt by their kinsmen in Ireland. And they had a determination to free Ireland from British rule far beyond the motivations of people in the Old Country. They provided the emotions and the cash that sustained every revolutionary and constitutional expression of Irish nationalism from the Fenian Brotherhood in the 1860s to the collapse of parliamentary Home Rule during World War I. Then the American Irish helped finance the Easter Week Rebellion in 1916 and the 1919-1921 Anglo-Irish War. And they also worked to create and organize the world opinion that persuaded Britain to concede Dominion status to three-fourths of Ireland. Some, but not many, Irish-Americans are still buying the guns and the explosives that have helped turn present day Northern Ireland into a living, blazing inferno.

Why did Irish-America hate Britain with a fanaticism that often exceeded love for Ireland? Many of the Irish were not successful in America. They came to the United States without technological skills and this frustrated their occupational mobility. Irish failure and Protestant prejudice fostered a paranoia that almost became genetic, particularly in New England. Poverty, oppression, and ghetto neuroses encouraged many Irish-Americans to distort their Irish backgrounds, to forget hard times in famine racked Ireland. In Irish-American memories and myths — the second and third generations were often more romantic about the Old Country than greenhorns — Ireland took on an emerald glow. They blamed the British for exiling them from their homeland, island paradise, and for their misery and failure in the United States.[7]

Not all Irish-American nationalism was a revelation of hate or neuroses. Some was the expression of American patriotism and much of it was a search for respectability in the United States. While the United States remained culturally Anglo-Saxon Protestant, the American Revolution and the War of 1812 left strong residues of anti-British feeling in American minds and hearts. Britain's pro-Confederate opinion and conduct during the Civil War served to prolong and intensify these sentiments. Irish-Americans who entered the United States as refugees from British misgovernment in Ireland naturally joined the anti-British public opinion consensus on American foreign policy. In the late nineteenth-century, when American governments began to imitate the practices of British imperialism and a large number of upper and middle class Americans embraced the Anglo-Saxon racist dogmas of British and American nativisms, United States foreign policy gradually retreated from its anti-British premises. In this changing situation, Irish-American leaders constantly attempted to frustrate rapproachment between the United States and the United Kingdom. Although their efforts proved considerably less successful than post-World War II strategies by other ethnics like the Greeks and Jews to shape American foreign policy, this failure was no reflection on the considerable political skills and the significant political power of the American Irish.[8] It only meant that Irish-American nationalism outlived Anglophilia in the United States, and in the twentieth-century the American Irish found themselves futilely trying to dismantle a mutually satisfactory Anglo-American alliance.

In searching for the sources of ethnic nationalism in the United States not enough attention is paid to the respectability motive. In "The Bent Twig—A Note on Nationalism," *Foreign Affairs,* October, 1972, Isaiah Berlin defined nationalism "as an expression of the inflamed desire of the insufficiently regarded to count for something among the cultures of the world." During the nineteenth and early twentieth-centuries, Irish-Americans were certainly among the "insufficiently regarded" members of American Society. Most of them who were not captives of the demoralizing, New England urban ghettos experienced economic mobility, moving up into the skilled working and lower middle classes — some even made it into the professional and upper middle classes. But as a group, Irish-Americans suffered from a nagging inferiority complex. Many of them concluded that Ireland in bondage to Britain·was the source of their "insufficiently regarded" status. They decided that an independent Irish nation state would win for them respect from other Americans. This conviction that there was a logical association between the liberation of Ireland and the success of Irish-America encouraged the American Irish to support a variety of Irish nationalist movements, constitutional and revolutionary. In equating an emancipated homeland with respectability in the United States, the Irish expressed an opinion that would be shared by other ethnic and religious minorities that followed them into the urban ghettos of America. Despite their failure to mobilize American foreign policy to free Ireland, the Irish pioneered the use of ethnic power to manipulate official American conduct in regard to other countries.

Since the 1921 Treaty between Britain and the Irish revolutionaries, Irish-Americans have gradually disassociated themselves from Irish nationalism. Most of them found the Irish Free State an acceptable British response to Irish demands for autonomy and a basis for an expansion of Irish sovereignty. The civil war in Ireland between the supporters of the Free State and those who insisted on a Republic completely separated from the British Commonwealth puzzled and disgusted many Irish-Americans. A decrease in physical and cultural relations between the Irish on either side of the Atlantic also weakened the concept of an international Irish community. Restrictions on immigration and the Great Depression of the late 1920s and early 1930s reduced the numbers of Irish people who entered the United States. Most of those who emigrated in the twentieth-century have gone to Britain where they found employment opportunities for unskilled laborers as well as for university trained professionals. Also life styles are closer to those back home, and inexpensive ship and air travel make it convenient to return to Ireland for Christmas and summer holidays.

After independence, post-Treaty Irish governments promoted

an exclusive Irish-Ireland brand of nationalism. Starting in the late 1950s, Irish political leaders without renouncing Irish-Ireland began to emphasize Ireland as a European nation. This policy culminated in Ireland joining the Common Market. Although the Gaelic Ireland and the European Community aspects of contemporary Irish nationalism are contradictory in spirit, they both reject close ties with the Irish of the diaspora who are deeply involved in the affairs of the English speaking world.

But the cultural separation between the Irish in Ireland and their kinsmen in the United States is a mutual rather than a one sided decision to follow different paths. Since the 1920s, the American Irish have passed through their identity crisis. They are no longer among the "insufficiently regarded" portion of American society, and as a result have lost their psychological dependence on Irish nationalism as a potential instrument of respectability. Except for a few isolated pockets of failure like South Boston, where personalities and perspectives have been warped by unpleasant historical experiences in both the Old and New Worlds, Irish-Americans have been freed from the task of assimilating and uplifting large numbers of new immigrants, and have evolved from an essentially working class to a middle class community whose influence is felt in all aspects of the economy and on the highest levels of government. The Irish are too successful in America to think much about Ireland. Very few of them have any knowledge of Irish history or literature. The response of most Irish-Americans to the current crisis in Northern Ireland illustrates the general indifference of the American Irish to Irish nationalism. Although Catholics in Northern Ireland suffer from the same kind of prejudice and poverty that early Irish immigrants experienced in urban America, most Irish-Americans do not understand why they agitate for civil rights or violently resist Protestant Ascendancy. The American Irish have lost or abandoned their historical memories. Similarities between the situation in Northern Ireland and the experience of their ancestors in nineteenth-century Ireland and America have not touched the minds or emotions of most of them.[9]

This volume contains four essays defining the Catholic and American dimensions of Irish nationalism. In "Irish Nationalism and Irish Catholicism: A Study in Cultural Identity," first published in *Church History*, December, 1973, I discuss the contradictions between the inclusive theory of Irish nationalism and its Catholic reality, emphasizing that Anglo-Saxon Protestant imperialism, colonialism, and nativism (in Ireland, Britain, and America) forced the Irish to build a national and cultural identity on Catholic foundations.

In "Nationalism and the Irish Peasant, 1800-1848," first published in *The Review of Politics,* October, 1953, and reprinted in 1971 as a volume in the American Committee for Irish Studies *Reprint Series* (editors Emmet Larkin and Lawrence J. McCaffrey), Thomas N. Brown, Professor of History at the University of Massachusetts - Boston, and the leading authority on Irish-American nationalism, describes how Daniel O'Connell's political and Young Ireland's cultural nationalisms failed to penetrate the minds of peasants more concerned with economic security than the achievement of an Irish nation state, more loyal to parishes and townlands than Ireland, and frightened of offending landlords who held the power of life and death over them. And this fear was mixed with hereditary allegiances to the class that represented British colonialism in Ireland. Brown points out how the Great Famine, 1845-1849, shattered the foundation of landlordism and speeded the process of emigration. He concludes that in urban American ghettos "the burden of Irish nationalism was to be borne for the next half-century; for in the alembic of America the parochial peasant was transformed into a passionate nationalist."

Brown's second essay, "The Origins and Character of Irish-American Nationalism," which also appeared originally in *The Review of Politics,* July 1956, details the influence of the American environment on the evolution of Irish nationalism. He asserts that Irish nationalism jelled in urban America and then sustained liberation movements back home. Brown portrays Irish-American nationalism as the product of immigrant loneliness, poverty, feelings of inferiority, and the search for respectability.

In his essay, "America and the Irish Problem, 1899-1921," first published in *Irish Historical Studies,* March, 1968, Alan J. Ward, Professor of Government at the College of William and Mary, and the leading expert on the Irish-American influence on Anglo-American relations, also argues that Irish poverty, psychological insecurity, irritated by Anglo-American Protestant nativism, brewed Irish-American nationalism. In this essay, Ward concentrates on the effectiveness of Irish-American leaders in injecting the Irish Question into Anglo-American relations from the time of the Boer War to the Treaty concluding the Anglo-Irish conflict. He shows how Irish-American nationalists, "influenced both public opinion and congress by leading and massively supporting attacks on Britain, by cultivating alliances with other groups hostile to Britain, by practicing a bellicose anglo-phobic Americanism, and by identifying themselves with traditional themes in American foreign policy, most notably non-alignment in the European balance of power and the inviolability of the western hemisphere — the Monroe doctrine." At a time when mutual imperialisms and Anglo-Saxon racist nativisms were bringing Britain and the United States closer together, Irish-American nationalism interrupted and delayed the process of rapprochment. Finally Irish-American tactics and pressures did influence Britain to concede Dominion status to most of Catholic nationalist Ireland, but it could not prevent the emergence of a strong Anglo-American alliance, and after the establishment of a Dominion status Irish Free State, Irish-American nationalism began to fade away.

Lawrence J. McCaffrey

Loyola University of Chicago
February, 1976

(1) Anglo-American and Anglo-Irish objections to British mercantilism and political domination shared the political philosophy of John Locke's *Treatise on Government* and the Glorious Revolution of 1688 as the intellectual source and the political precedent for their protest movements. And Anglo-Irish patriots exploited the American Revolution to demand and win free trade and a sovereign parliament from Britain.

(2) Many revolutionary Irish nationalists trace their tradition back to the United Irishmen and their 1798 rebellion. But the United Irishmen were also in the general European intellectual stream advocating the more radical political theories that emerged from the Enlightment — Rousseau, Paine, and Jefferson. They were an Irish version of the French Jacobins and found inspiration in the French Revolution.

(3) Many Irish nationalists would argue that their movement was inclusive rather than exclusive, inviting the participation of Anglo-Irish Protestants as well as Catholic Celts. This thesis has recently come under challenge from Ailfrid MacLochlainn, Deputy Director of the National Library of Ireland. In a paper, "Thomas Davis and Irish Racialism," presented to the 1975 American Committee for Irish Studies meeting at Stonehill College, Easton, Massachusetts, on April 25, MacLochlainn claimed that contrary to the ecumenical front projected by Young Ireland, Thomas Davis' interpretation of Irish history in poems and essays published in the *Nation* encouraged racial distinctions and animosity between native Catholics and Anglo-Irish Protestants. In another revisionist paper, Maurice O'Connell, Professor of History at Fordham University, told a regional meeting of the American Catholic Historical Association at Boston College on April 5, 1975 that Davis encouraged religious and class divisions between Irish Catholics and Protestants. It is quite obvious that the emphasis on a Gaelic or Irish-Ireland meant an exclusive Catholic nationalism since the vast majority of Irish Protestants identified with an English rather than Irish speaking cultural background. The twentieth-century slogan "Ireland free, united, and Gaelic" is a contradiction in terms since it automatically excludes Ulster Protestants who are hostile to any notion of a Gaelic Ireland.

(4) Irish nationalists honor a number of Protestants among the heroes of their nation. Among the most prominent are Henry Grattan, the leader of the Protestant patriot movement in the 1770s and 1780s, enemy of the Union, friend of Catholic Emancipation; Theobold Wolfe Tone, co-founder of the Society of United Irishmen, champion of an ecumenical Irish nation; Robert Emmet who died for Irish freedom in 1803 after making a speech calling on subsequent generations to take up his cause; Thomas Davis, co-founder and ideologist of Young Ireland; William Smith O'Brien, a leader of the 1848 rebellion; John Mitchel, radical Young Irelander, passionate journalist of Irish liberty; Isaac Butt, founder of the Home Rule movement; Charles Stewart Parnell who perfected Butt's idea and made the Irish Parliamentary Party a dominant force in Irish and British politics in the 1880s; Standish O'Grady and Douglas Hyde, scholarly founding fathers of the Gaelic language movement; literary geniuses like Johnathan Swift, William Butler Yeats; Lady Augusta Gregory, John Millington Synge, Sean O'Casey; and Erskine Childers who gave up the comfortable life of the Anglo-Irish gentry to die as an Irish rebel, and his son Erskine who became the fourth President of the Irish Republic.

The liberal spirit of the Catholic majority in the South is in remarkable contrast to the bigotry of the Protestant majority in the North, but this praise deserves some qualification. Perhaps if the Catholic minority in the North was only five percent like the Protestant minority in the South, Catholics in the Six Counties might have resigned themselves to a divided Ireland, and Protestants might have felt less insecure and more tolerant. And it must be remembered that the Irish Free State and the Irish Republic have both been Catholic confessional nation states. Until quite recently, Catholicism enjoyed a favored religion status in the Constitution, and Irish Catholic notions of family and sexual morality still dominate law and custom.

(5) Many Irish nationalists will dispute my position on the intolerance of Anglo-Irish patriots pointing to the United Irishmen to prove their case. It is true that the United Irishmen did advocate religious tolerance, supported Catholic Emancipation, and projected an Irish Republic where all citizens would be equal. But the United Irishmen did not represent majority Irish opinion. People like Theobold Wolfe Tone, one of the founders of the United Irishmen, were really Deists with a contempt for all forms of organized religion. This attitude separated them from both Protestant and Catholic opinion. The theories of the United Irishmen had little impact on Catholic rebels in 1798 who fought as a peasant protest against landlordism and most Ulster Protestant United Irishmen had no interest in elevating the condition of their Catholic fellow countrymen. The superficial strength of United Irishmen ideology was demonstrated by the popularity of the Orange Order in Ulster after the collapse of the 1798 rebellions. For an excellent evaluation of the true character and strength of the United Irishmen and the motivations for rebellion in Wexford, Antrim, Down and the West in 1798 see Robert Kee, *The Green Flag* (New York: Delacorte, 1972).

(6) The futile effort of Catholic nationalists to court Protestants whose historical traditions, cultural identity, and economic and political self-interest determined a loyalty to the British connection severely restricted the ideology of Irish nationalism, depriving it of an economic dimension. Many Irish nationalists were economic radicals who realized the potential of the land question as an instrument to radicalize the Irish masses, but they shied away from emphasizing the agrarian issue because it might antagonize potential Protestant recruits for nationalism.

(7) John Mitchel, the most passionate of Young Irelanders, an exile who eventually found a home in the United States, articulated the hate factor in Irish nationalism as follows:

"I have found that there was perhaps
less of love in it than of hate —
less of filial affection to my country than of scournful impatience at the
thought that I had the misfortune,
I and my children, to be born in a
country which suffered itself to be
oppressed and humiliated by another . . .
And hatred being the thing I chiefly
cherished and cultivated, the thing
which I specially hated was the British
system . . . wishing always that I could
strike it between wind and water and
shiver its timbers."

(quoted in Thomas Flanagan's essay "John Mitchel and the Jail Journal," *Irish University Review,* Autumn, 1970, pp. 4-5).

(8) In explaining his difficulties in persuading the United States to support Britain more actively in World War I, the United Kingdom Ambassador to the United States, Sir Cecil Spring-Rice wrote his Foreign Secretary, Sir Edward Grey, that he was checked by Irish-American leaders who "had unequaled power of organization" and were "the best politicians in the country." (Alan J. Ward, *Ireland and Anglo-American Relations, 1899-1921,* Toronto: University of Toronto Press, 1969, pp. 94,95).

(9) In the Republic of Ireland the combined strength of the Provisional and Official wings of the IRA represents only about three percent of public opinion as measured in local election results. Even in Northern Ireland where many people regard the IRA as a Catholic defense force protecting their community from Protestant Loyalist and British army violence, a significant majority of Catholics prefer the leadership of the parliamentary Social Democratic Labour Party. In the United States, IRA support is also very small in the Irish-American community. But the IRA makes so much noise that its significance is exaggerated. Many Irish-Americans donate money to IRA front groups thinking that their money will be used for humanitarian causes in the Six Counties, not realizing that they are helping to purchase guns and explosives that will kill Irish men, women, and children. A large number of people who do join American IRA front organizations represent the residues of paranoia that formerly afflicted the ghetto Irish. Some of them are recently arrived immigrants who have not really moved into the middle class status enjoyed by most Irish-Americans, others are American born, but still entertain the persecution mentality of their ancestors. In Britain they can locate a target for their frustration. Britain is responsible for the mess in Northern Ireland — it is the fruits of centuries of British policy in Ireland — but rational people realize that British withdrawal will lead to civil war — the slaughter of Catholics and Protestants — rather than unity. And the violence and hatred that will emerge from civil war will postpone the achievement of a united Ireland farther into the future.

NATIONALISM AND THE IRISH PEASANT, 1800-1848

Thomas N. Brown

Nationalism and the Irish Peasant, 1800-1848

by Thomas N. Brown

> Pleased and contented with what fortune gives,
> Free from ambition and pride he lives,
> His bosom with no fine ideas fraught,
> But to the sluggish hearth chained every thought.
> "The Peasant," *Anthologia Hibernica*—June, 1793

The Old Order

IN the years preceding the Great Famine the people of Ireland were separated in space and spirit by the divisive workings of history and geography and by the survival of ancient local customs that were feudal and in some instances, tribal in origin. In 1825, according to a contemporary observer, there were "different districts in Ireland almost as unlike each other as any two countries in Europe."[1] A thousand light years and more separated the Georgian splendor of Dublin from the rude Gaelic society of the West. And in all the provinces there were pockets where distinctive local cultures stubbornly endured; like the baronies of Bargy and Forth, in the extreme southeast corner of Wexford, whose inhabitants clung to a Chaucerian dialect until the middle of the century, or the fishing village of Claddagh, outside the city of Galway, where the people maintained a severe aloofness, marrying among themselves and ignoring outsiders.[2]

Living out his life within the narrow orbit of the parish, according to the slow rhythm of the seasons,[3] the peasant looked suspiciously upon the stranger from the world outside. To the Gael of Connemara, that once romantic and primitive district

---

[1] Testimony of John Leslie Foster, M.P., before a Committee of the House of Lords, quoted in George Cornwall Lewis, *On Local Disturbances in Ireland* (London, 1836), 75.

[2] For traveler's impressions see Constantia Maxwell, *Country and Town in Ireland under the Georges* (Dublin, 1949) 144-147. See also Henry D. Inglis, *Journey Throughout Ireland in the Summer and Autumn of 1834* (London, 1836), 26-27, and Johan George Kohl, *Ireland* (New York, 1844), 57. For the Claddagh district, see Inglis, *ibid.*, 214-215.

[3] See Thomas Crofton Croker, *Researches in the South of Ireland* (London, 1824), 221-222 and E. Estyn Evans, *Irish Heritage* (Dundalk, 1942 *passim;* "A Cosmopolite," *The Sportsman in Ireland* (London, 1840), II, 32-33.

of Connacht, lying between Lough Corrib and the Atlantic, the people of Leinster were hostile "Saxons";[4] and the Connacht man in the eyes of the peasantry from the other provinces was a rude and obstreperous bog-trotter.[5] The Connacht peasants, according to Archbishop Croke, could "no more migrate from one county to another than from Ireland to America; where they were born they would die; a Connaught man would be chased out of Munster like a fox by the Munster men."[6]

Though Irish roads were not inferior to those of England, and the coach system developed by the Italian, Charles Bianconi, linked together the main towns, innumerable smaller towns and villages could only be reached by ragged boreens.[7] Rugged mountains and treacherous bogs effectively sealed off much of the West, as Maria Edgeworth discovered when she made her hazardous journey into Connemara in 1833.[8] And in the 1820's a Dubliner could communicate more quickly with Daniel O'Connell's native Iveragh on the Kerry coast by sending a letter by ship via America, rather than by dispatching it the one hundred and sixty Irish miles overland.[9] Even when communication was possible the Irish seemed disposed to remain aloof. When the Bishop of Cloyne appeared before a House of Commons Committee investigating discontent in Ireland in 1867, he reluctantly admitted that, though he had travelled widely on the continent, he had never been in the counties of Wicklow and Wexford.[10]

The commercial wealth of Belfast and the respectable farms of the surrounding districts presented a sharp contrast to the meanness of much of the middle counties and the extreme pov-

---

[4] Constantia Maxwell, *op. cit.*, 140.

[5] Barbara M. Kerr, "Irish Seasonal Migration to Great Britain, 1800-1838", *Irish Historical Studies*, vol. III, (1942-3), 369.

[6] In Wilfrid Seawen Blunt, *The Land War in Ireland* (London, 1912), 98.

[7] Constantia Maxwell, *op. cit.*, 294; W. Bence Jones, *The Life's Work in Ireland of a Landlord who Tried to Do His Duty* (London, 1880), 29.

[8] Maria Edgeworth, *Tour in Connemara*, edited with introduction and notes by Harold Edgeworth Butler (London, 1951). See also W. H. Maxwell, *Wild Sports of the West*, Every Irishman's Library edition (London, n.d.), passim.

[9] Constantia Maxwell, *op. cit.*, 294.

[10] *Report From the Select Committee on Tenure and Improvement of Land* (Ireland) *Act; together with the Proceedings of the Committees, Minutes of Evidence, Appendix and Index* (House of Commons, 1865), 184. Cited hereafter as *Report Select Committee Tenure Ireland, Act, 1865.*

erty of the South and Southwest.[11] But Ulster itself was hardly homogeneous. The Catholic mountain districts of Donegal, like most of Ireland, did not share in the benefits which the Act of Union conferred upon Presbyterian Belfast.[12] The feeling of tolerance which had developed during the latter half of the eighteenth century between Catholic and Protestant had gone to smash when increasing installments of Catholic emancipation from the Penal Laws thrust the Catholic farmer into sharp competition with Protestants for the farms of the North.[13] The two clashed in 1795 at the memorable Battle of the Diamond and the blood which flowed revived and intensified old hatreds. These hatreds were institutionalized in the Orange Society, organized after the battle and fanatically devoted to perpetuating Hanoverian rule in England and the Protestant Ascendancy in Ireland and in the society of Ribbonmen, formed by the lower orders of Catholics to resist Orange aggression. While the Orange order enjoyed aristocratic favor for many years, notably from the Duke of Cumberland, Ribbonmen were denounced by all, Catholic and Protestant alike.[14]

Religious differences were not the only barriers to the generation of national feeling in Ireland. Equally divisive was the spirit of faction or clanship. Factions were made up of groups, loosely allied through kinship, in whom ancestral pride and love of combat were so strong that year after year they would fight with hostile factions at fairs and "patterns" (religious pilgrimages), or

---

[11] See Report of the Railway Commission, appointed in 1836 to consider establishment of railroads in Ireland, in R. Barry O'Brien, *Thomas Drummond, Life and Letters* (London, 1889), 290-297. Also Jonathan Pim, *The Conditions and Prospects of Ireland* (Dublin, 1848), 18-23.

[12] Eric Strauss, *Irish Nationalism and British Democracy* (New York, 1951), 76; George O'Brien, *The Economic History of Ireland From the Union to the Famine* (London, 1921), 579.

[13] William Edward Hartpole Lecky, *A History of Ireland in the Eighteenth Century* (London, 1912), II, 506-511, III. 399-400. George Cornewall Lewis, *op. cit.*, 36-37.

[14] For the origin of Ribbon and Orange orders see Lecky, *op. cit.*, vol. III, 421-429. R. Barry O'Brien, *op. cit.*, 96-195. For opposition of Catholic priests to Ribbonmen see David Leahy, ed., *An Abstract of the Evidence Taken Before the Committee of the House of Lords Upon the State of Crime in Ireland During the Period From June, 1835 to January, 1839* (London, 1839), 43. See also testimony of Daniel O'Connell in Lewis, *op. cit.*, 156 for his hatred and fear of Ribbonmen.

wherever they met in sufficient numbers.[15] Sometimes the origin of the feud was forgotten. The famous feud between the Dignen and Dawson factions of Tipperary arose over a quarrel as to the proper burial place for a woman whose marriage had temporarily united both clans.[16] The traveller Inglis, in commenting upon faction fights, perhaps exaggerated when he wrote that "the O'Sullivans are as distinct a people from the O'Neills as the Dutch from the Belgians."[17] But there can be little doubt about the antagonisms aroused by the fights.[18] As many as five hundred people were known to have taken part in them, using gun butts and shillelaghs as weapons; and in what turned out to be the last great faction fight, held at Rathkenny in 1832, over forty persons were drowned.[19] After that time Thomas Drummond, Chief Secretary for Ireland during the Whig ministry of Lord Melbourne, realizing that the feuds were often conducted under the patronage of the resident magistrates, brought the fights under control through the use of itinerant magistrates and a reorganized constabulary.[20]

Clan feeling made the administration of law, according to Anglo-Saxon concepts, extremely difficult in Ireland, giving the Irish people an unenviable reputation for lawlessness and prevarication. Without doubt disrespect for English law stemmed in part from the fact that English law was more often an instrument of oppression for the Irish peasant in the first part of the nineteenth century than one of justice. Despite, however, the example of the Lynch of Galway who in the fifteenth century put his own son to death for a crime, conceptions of corporate virtue have made little headway to this day with a people whose dearest

---

[15] Constantia Maxwell, *op. cit.*, 156-158; Lewis, *op. cit.*, 279-297; R. B. O'Brien, *op. cit.*, 247.

[16] Lewis, *op. cit.*, 288; R. B. O'Brien, *op. cit.*, 247-249.

[17] Inglis, *op. cit.*, 161.

[18] See the comments of the Gaelic diarist, Humphrey O'Sullivan in *The Diary of Humphrey O'Sullivan*, Michael McGrath, editor and translator. XXXIII, 161, Irish Texts Society (Dublin, 1937), part IV, 31, 45.

[19] Lewis, *Ibid.; Sportsman in Ireland*, I, 186.

[20] For Drummond's work see R. B. O'Brien, *op. cit.*, 285; R. B. O'Brien, *Dublin Castle and the Irish People* (London, 1909), 114-118. Also Leahy, *op. cit.*, 93-96, 137-138. See Lewis, *op. cit.*, 286-287 for patronage of factions by resident magistrates.

loyalties remain familial.[21] "To save a relation from punishment, or to punish anyone who has injured a relation, an Irish peasant will swear to anything," was the conclusion of Inglis, after witnessing some extraordinary scenes at the Longford and Clare assizes.[22] Matthew Barrington, landlord and magistrate, thought that a sense of chivalry prevented an Irishman from testifying against a friend.[23]

The Irish peasant was caught between two worlds. He clung to a social code derived from the past when he could look to his lord or chieftain to "defend him in his just and unjust causes."[24] Deprived of such support in the modern law court, the peasant found himself bound to testify against his own. To extract himself from this predicament, he often resorted to an ingenious casuistry, devising elaborate false oaths, and often, when all else failed, retreating into the bewildering labyrinths of the Gaelic language.[25]

Traditional feudal loyalties and attitudes bound the tenant to the landlord, inhibiting the growth of more abstract national allegiances. And feudalism was a long time dying in Ireland. While memories of the bondage endured under the Penal Laws perpetuated peasant distrust of the Protestant gentry and the savage repression of the Revolution of 1798 and the consequent Act of Union in 1800 left deep scars of bitterness,[26] other forces were at work to bind peasant and lord together. Even the withdrawal from Ireland of many of the richest aristocrats after the Act of

---

[21] For an illuminating discussion of this point see Conrad Arensberg *The Irish Countryman* (New York, 1937).

[22] Inglis, *op. cit.,* 162.

[23] Lewis, *op. cit.,* 253.

[24] Gerard Murphy, "The Gaelic Background" in *Daniel O'Connell: Nine Centenary Essays,* Michael Tierney, ed. (Dublin, 1949), II. See also W. H. Maxwell, *op. cit.,* 357-365; Sir Jonah Barrington, *Personal Sketches of His Own Time,* 2 vols. (Philadelphia, 1827), II, 31-32.

[25] See William Carleton, "An Essay on Irish Swearing," in his *Traits and Stories of the Irish Peasantry.* D. J. O'Donoghue, ed. (London, 1846), 4 vols., I, 203-219 for typical false oaths. Also Inglis, *op. cit.,* 165-167 and Croker, *op. cit.,* 228-229. O'Connell, a master of equivocal language himself, expressed concern about "the awful flippancy of oath-taking and the horrid crime of perjury" in letter of November 10, 1844 to Dr. Gray. See William J. Fitzpatrick, *Correspondence of Daniel O'Connell, the Liberator,* (New York, 1888) 2 vols., II, 346-348.

[26] Constantia Maxwell, *op. cit.,* 179.

Union, so bitterly criticized then and now, helped to preserve their prestige. For the miseries of tenant and cottier were blamed upon the hated middlemen, who managed the land, and the illusion cherished that all would be well were the noble absentee to return.[27]

Though the political influence of the landed aristocracy was on the decline throughout the whole of the nineteenth century, they retained great influence and control in the administration of county affairs. Jurors, chosen from among the gentry by the sheriff, decided the county rates and returned indictments in criminal cases as well. The Protestant rector, inspector of police, and resident magistrate were the landlord's intimates and the estate agent and steward his hirelings.[28] He held the reins of power and in the words of Lord Clare, "a landlord of straw could grind to powder a tenant of steel."[29]

Landlords also served as Justices of the Peace and discharged that function in ways both arbitrary and colorful. The various and complex systems of land tenure in Ireland gave rise to an extraordinary amount of litigation.[30] Because experience had taught the Irish to distrust the impartial working of the law, they sought justice through influence. " 'I'll have the law of you' is the saying of an Englishman who expects justice," observed shrewd Maria Edgeworth. " 'I'll have you up before his honor,' is the threat of an Irishman who hopes for partiality."[31]

The landlord also kept a grip on the peasantry through the manorial courts, whose jurisdiction in cases of petty claims, sometimes covered entire baronies. The Seneschal of the court, often venal and corrupt, was appointed by the lord of the manor. In some instances where the manor had been alienated the privilege

---

[27] *Digest of Evidence Taken Before Her Majesty's Commissioners of Inquiry into the State of the Law and Practice in Respect to Occupation of Land in Ireland* (cited hereafter as Devon Comm.) 2 vols. (Dublin, 1847-48), I, 337-338. Also Maria Edgeworth, *The Absentees.* The English Comedie Humaine Edition (New York, 1904), 152-153.

[28] L. Paul-Dubois, *Contemporary Ireland* (Dublin, 1911), 94, 193.

[29] Quoted by Daniel O'Connell to Devon Commission. *Devon Commission,* II, 835.

[30] Inglis, *op. cit.,* 381; Evans, *op. cit.,* 52.

[31] Constantia Maxwell, *op. cit.,* 182, quoted from *The Absentees.*

of conducting the court remained with the former owner.[32]

The overwhelming balance of power in their favor developed in the Protestant gentry an arrogance that was given great dimensions by the almost enracinated sense of inferiority felt by Catholics. "They keep us like slaves, and then they despise us," a young Irishman told the American reformer, Mrs. Asenath Nicholson, in 1845.[33] Vestiges of subservience even clung to so influential a figure as Michael Davitt. When he was at the height of his power in 1882, at a critical moment in his relationship with the aristocratic Charles Stuart Parnell, Davitt told an audience of Irish-Americans that because he was only a peasant he could not seriously consider challenging the leadership of Parnell.[34]

It was more than habit and folk memory that made sycophants of Catholics. For the Catholic farmer was utterly dependent for his holding upon the goodwill of the landlord, especially so after the emancipation of Catholics in 1829, when the threat of a politically independent tenantry moved landlords to refuse long leases that would qualify tenants as ten pound freeholders.[35] And, as Justin McCarthy once truly said, "The land is the love, but it is also the life of the Irish people."[36]

The terrible need for the benediction of the gentry immobilized the farmer. Aware of this, Irish reformers sought repeatedly to penetrate and control local judicial and administrative offices.[37]

---

[32] See Report from the *Select Committee on Manor Courts in Ireland Together with Minutes of Evidence* (n.p., 1837), passim.

[33] Sean O'Faolain, *King of the Beggars* (New York, 1938), 141. Also *ibid.*, 141-147. Also Charles Gavan Duffy, *Young Ireland: A Fragment of Irish History.* (New York, 1881), 71, 144; C. Maxwell, *op. cit.*, 176-178. Gustave De Beaumont, *Ireland: Social, Political and Religious* (Dublin, 1839), vol. II, 16-17.

[34] William O'Brien, *Recollections* (London, 1905), 446. See also *Irish World*, July 1, 1882, where he is quoted as saying in New York's Academy of Music: "The Irish people would never accept me as a leader because I belong to the ranks of the people."

[35] *Report Select Committee Tenure Ireland Act, 1865*, 184; *Devon Commission*, II, 1121; David Bennett King, *The Irish Question* (New York, 1882), 35.

[36] Norman Dunbar Palmer, *The Irish Land League Crisis* (New Haven, 1940), 2.

[37] O'Connell achieved borough reform, being himself elected Lord Mayor of Dublin in 1838. He was also instrumental in bringing Thomas Drummond to Ireland, who instructed landlords that they had duties as well as rights, and whose stipendiary magistrates curbed landlord power. See

When this proved unsatisfactory nationalists took the more radical step of setting up courts independent of the government.[38] When tenants were asked to defy their landlords in 1826 and in the 1880's efforts were made to compensate them for whatever losses they suffered.[39] Not, however, until the English Parliament threw its support to the tenantry in the 1880's was sufficient countervailing power built up against the landlords and the feudal bonds finally loosened.

Nevertheless, feudalism in Ireland in the years before the Famine was dying. In the Catholic Emancipation fight tenants repeatedly broke with their landlords by voting for candidates pledged to the Catholic Association. Having long considered the tenant vote to be a proprietary right, landlords were shocked and frightened by this emergence of Democracy.[40] Lord Sligo in disgust quit Ireland for Jamaica.[41] And Lord Kingston ("Big George," as he was called), benevolent despot of estates in Cork, Tipperary, and Limerick and sovereign in the town of Mitchelstown, called the tenants to his massive castle after they had dared to elect to Parliament a candidate whom he had opposed. Before the mob, assembled in the hundred-foot-long castle gallery Big George suddenly and surprisingly went mad. "They are come to tear me to pieces," he cried again and again.[42] Big George sur-

---

R. Barry O'Brien, *Thomas Drummond*, 273-287. After Drummond's death stipendiary magistrates no longer served this purpose. R. Barry O'Brien, *Dublin Castle and the Irish People*, 114-118. Basic also to the program of the New Departure in 1878, often erroneously assumed to mean simply Fenian support of land agitation, was the infiltration of local administrative bodies by nationalists. See John Devoy's letters to the Dublin's *Freeman's Journal* printed in part in Boston *Pilot*, January 18, 1879 and *Irish World*, November 9, 1878.

[38] The repeal Association set up Arbitration Courts, headed by magistrates dismissed for sympathy to Repeal. Duffy, *Young Ireland*, 304. The Land League set up similar courts, see Palmer, *op. cit.*, 167. So too did the Sein Feiners.

[39] See Thomas Wyse, *Historical Sketch of the Late Catholic Association of Ireland*. 2 vols. (London, 1829). vol. I, 295 and see "objects" of Mayo Land League in Michael Davitt, *The Fall of Feudalism in Ireland* (London, 1904), 162-163, and King, *op. cit.*, 122.

[40] Inglis, *op. cit.*, 257; Extracts from "Monsieur Duvergier's Letters on the State of Ireland, 1826." Letter II. In Wyse, *op. cit.*, vol. II, Appendix no. xvii, lii-liii: Godfrey Locker-Lampson, *A Consideration of the State of Ireland in the Nineteenth Century* (London, 1907), 121.

[41] Inglis, *op. cit.*, 257.

[42] Elizabeth Bowen, *Bowen's Court* (New York, 1942), 257-258.

rendered too early. Not until the 1860's and 1870's could the nationalists claim to have seriously undermined the political power of the gentry.[43]

Yet even in Connemara—the land "geographically west of the law,"[44] where the Martins of Ballinahinch ruled over half a million acres with oppressive vigor, the old order was in decay. The "reign" of Thomas Martin, like that of other earlier chieftains, depended upon the ability to perpetuate among the people the legend that in their illicit smuggling and distilling they need have no fear of the king's writ.[45] When Thomas Martin was himself arrested in 1838 for leading his ragged tenants into battle with the men of O'Flaherty for possession of a disputed piece of land, clearly his archaic rule was coming to an end. Like Big George Thomas Martin was a victim of the forces of modernity. He died in 1847 of Famine Fever, contracted in the finest traditions of his class while visiting his starving tenantry in the poorhouse. And with so many of the great holdings, the Martin Estate was mired in debt, and after Martin's death, passed into the hands of the Encumbered Estates Court, to eventually become the plaything of an Indian prince and polo player.[46]

Forces of Change

The most powerful solvents of the feudal order in rural Ireland were the economic forces working from the latter half of the eighteenth century onward to assimilate the economy of Ireland into that of England's. By 1825 Irish manufacturing and domestic industry, outside of the Ulster area, were dead or dying, and

[43] William O'Brien, op. cit., 103-105; Mark F. Ryan, Fenian Memories (Dublin, 1945), 42-44.

[44] Edgar L. Wakefield in Boston Pilot, February 9, 1889; A traditional view. See Lecky, op. cit., II, 357 ff; Inglis, op. cit., 238.

[45] W. H. Maxwell, op. cit., 146; Murphy, op. cit., passim; O'Faolain, op. cit., 145-147; Constantia Maxwell, op. cit., 179.

[46] Edgeworth, Tour in Connemara, passim. For descriptions of these great feudal families see Lecky, op. cit., vol. III, 415-418; James Anthony Froude, The English in Ireland in the Eighteenth Century. 3 vols. (New York, 1873), vol. I, 447-500; Daniel Corkery, The Hidden Ireland: A Study of Gaelic Munster in the Eighteenth Century (Dublin, 1925), 30-58; Constantia Maxwell, op. cit., 176-218.

Irish agriculture was at the mercy of a ruthless English market.[47] Whether it was grain or beef that that Moloch demanded, the small Irish farmer and his laborer, the cottier, could only supply them by subsisting themselves almost exclusively on a diet of potatoes.[48]

Feudal values were replaced by those of commerce, under the pressure of the English market. Big House hospitality and peasant loyalty broke down, when money payments replaced the old payments in kind, and the handling of gold often transformed an old patriarch into a rapacious rackrenter.[49]

In an ancient Irish joke presence of the family pig in the cabin is defended as being eminently fair since, after all, he is the gentleman who pays the rent. As the nineteenth century wore on, and the pig became a luxury few Irish farmers could afford, the irony of the joke became increasingly tragic.[50] Assimilation of the economies of Ireland and England was completed in the first quarter of a century following the Act of Union and its fruits were poverty, bitterness and chronic violence.

In the first part of the eighteenth century Irish farm produce was smuggled abroad or consumed at home. With the growth of **English factory towns in the latter** half of the century, Ireland was afforded a profitable grain market and after the passage of Foster's Corn Law in 1784 a protected one, so that Irish grazing lands were increasingly plowed up into tillage farms.[51] When food prices ballooned upward during the Napoleonic wars, leaseholders found it more profitable to sublet rather than to work the land.[52] Between the landlord, living perhaps in Dublin or London, and the vast swarms of peasantry working the land, there grew up a parasitic class of middlemen who sucked the blood of

---

[47] Strauss, *op. cit.*, 75-79; George O'Brien, *op. cit.*, 578-579. William Forbes Adams, *Ireland and Irish Emigration to the New World From 1815 to the Famine* (New Haven, 1932), 135-136.

[48] George O'Brien, *op. cit.*, 21-26; Oscar Handlin *Boston's Immigrants, 1790-1865* (Cambridge, Mass., 1941), 44.

[49] Murphy, *op. cit.*, 18.

[50] Inglis, *op. cit.*, 45; Strauss, *op. cit.*, 82.

[51] G. O'Brien, *op. cit.*, 43-44; Strauss, *op. cit.*, 77, 79.

[52] G. O'Brien, *ibid.;* Strauss, *op. cit.*, 80-81; Constantia Maxwell, *op. cit.*, 135.

both.[53] When Grattan's Parliament in 1793 gave the franchise to the forty-shilling freeholder, it furnished the landlord with an additional motive for indifference toward the evil of subletting, for, as noted earlier, the vote of the tenant was assumed to be the property of the landlord.[54]

The potato, cheaply and easily grown, made possible the rapid increase of the peasantry that almost tripled the population of Ireland between 1785 and 1841.[55] Because Ireland lacked the industries to absorb this increase and emigration, except to England, being impossible for most, the farmer had no choice but to divide his already minutely divided holdings among his children.[56] "Every patch produces a new family," wrote an observer in 1822, "every member of a family a new patch . . . . hence a country covered with beggars—a complete pauper warren."[57] The potato, however, was a poor thing upon which to erect a society. The very ease with which it was grown helped to breed that improvident and devil-may-care attitude characteristic of Irish society during the "gap in the famines," between 1741 and 1822.[58] And when the potato blight struck, and the foul stench from the rotting plants settled over the countryside, as happened in 1822, 1831, 1835, and 1836, 1837 and then catastrophically in 1845, the people starved.[59] Even in normally healthy years the potato alone was insufficient to sustain life in the West of Ireland. From early in the eighteenth century it had been customary for small bands of peasants from the West and South, after the potato stock was exhausted in the summer, to migrate to England and Scotland for work in the harvest fields. Others went over to work on the canals and railroads, or to serve as laborers in the building trades. Prolonged depression in Ireland and cheap steamboat service to

[53] G. O'Brien, *op. cit.*, 44; Constantia Maxwell, *op. cit.*, 114; Lecky, *op. cit.*, III, 404; Inglis, *op. cit.*, 210-211.

[54] *Infra*, 10.

[55] From 2,845,932 to 8,175,124. Barbara M. Kerr, "Irish Seasonal Migration to Great Britain, 1800-1838," in *Irish Historical Studies*, III, 1942, 43,367. See also Constantia Maxwell, *op. cit.*, 119; Evans, *op. cit.*, 35.

[56] Handlin, *op. cit.*, 47-48; Adams, *op. cit.*, 104-105.

[57] In George O'Brien, *op. cit.*, 46-47, *The State of the Nation* (London, 1822).

[58] Kerr, *loc. cit.*, 368; Handlin, *op. cit's.*, 46; George O'Brien, *op. cit.*, 31ff.

[59] Locker-Lampson, *op. cit.*, 270.

England after 1816 increased the number of spalpeens, as the migratory workers were called; in 1841 over 57,000 crossed over to Scotland and England.[60] While the spalpeen was gone, his cabin was padlocked and his family sent begging along the road.[61] On his way he might meet with insult from peasants of Leinster, suspicion of his intentions, or with stones thrown in resentment by English laborers, who feared competition;[62] but in September he would return with wages sewn inside his shirt and perhaps too with unsettling ideas derived from the wide world beyond the Shannon.[63]

The landlords remained indifferent to the dangerous build-up of population until grain prices tumbled at the close of the Napoleonic wars. Then, anxious to convert tillage land to pasture, or to practice more efficient grain production, they began to clear off the peasantry and consolidate holdings.[64] Their zeal for this was tempered somewhat by the political value of the tenant; moreover, to evict him, without offering him a place to go, could be dangerous.[65] By the 1840's these restraints had disappeared; the forty-shilling freeholder lost the franchise in 1829 and the Poor Law of 1838 provided ways to subsidize emigration.[66]

The great clearances came during the Famine, which dragged the land from 1845 to 1850. To many landlords, impressed by the dogmas of utilitarian economics, the tragic inability of the tenants to pay their rents in these years offered a unique opportunity to rid themselves of their burdensome and backward tenantry.[67] To many Whig and Radical members of Parliament,

---

[60] Handlin, *op. cit.*, 47-48; Inglis, *op. cit.*, 200; Kerr, *loc. cit.*, 370-375.
[61] Inglis, *ibid.*
[62] Kerr, *loc. cit.*, 369-375.
[63] Kerr, *loc. cit.*, 370—argues that spalpeens had too little contact with English workers to be influenced by them and that whatever their ideas of the comparative comfort of the English laborer they had no opportunity to apply them. But see the *Sportsman in Ireland*, vol. I, 144-147, for story of Kerry mountaineer who learned about O'Connell and Irish politics as spalpeen. Also Lewis, *op. cit.*, 109-110, and W. J. Fitzpatrick, *The Life, Times and Correspondence of the Right Rev. Dr. Doyle* (Dublin, 1880), II, 238.
[64] Strauss, *op. cit.*, 81; O'Brien, *op. cit.*, 52-53; Handlin, *op. cit.*, 49.
[65] Handlin, *op. cit.*, 50.
[66] Handlin, *ibid.*; Strauss, *op. cit.*, 81-82.
[67] Handlin, *op. cit.*, 50-51; Strauss, *op. cit.*, 135-138; Pim, *op. cit.*, 58-59; Asenath Nicholson. *Annals of the Famine in Ireland* (New York 1851), 180-181.

influenced by the same dogmas, the Famine offered an opportunity to rid Ireland of the debt-ridden, devil-may-care landlord as well.[68] Subsidized emigration and the Encumbered Estates Act, passed in 1849 to facilitate sale of estates burdened by debts, were designed to replace the uneconomic tenant and landlord with "capitalist profit-producers."[69] Between 1841 and 1849 "dwarf farms" of five acres or less were reduced in number from 444,750 to 130,618 and over a million persons were evicted.[70] In the first thirty years of operation of the encumbered estates courts, roughly one-fourth of the land of Ireland changed hands, with the majority of the new landlords coming from the Irish business community.[71]

The new landlords were on the whole a disappointment. Made up largely of shopkeepers, attorneys and "gombeen men" (village usurers), with little spare capital and so "forced to farm out of the till,"[72] they failed to improve their estates and to stimulate capital investment in Ireland to any significant degree.[73] Like the speculating middlemen of the eighteenth century, these landlords recruited from the bourgeoisie were uninhibited in their pursuit of profits by considerations of ancestral loyalty or peasant custom. Only in the exaction of rent were they more efficient than the gentry they displaced. The tenant farmer despised them and looked back nostalgically to the days before the Famine when the old families owned the land.[74]

Unlike the early speculators, however, who served as a kind of

---

[68] Strauss, *ibid.;* Locker-Lampson, *op. cit.,* 263.

[69] Strauss, *op. cit.,* 136.

[70] Handlin, *op. cit.,* 51.   For different estimates see Locker-Lampson, *op. cit.,* 275; Strauss, *op. cit.,* 137; John E. Pomfret, *The Struggle for Land in Ireland,* 1800-1923 (Princeton, New Jersey, 1923), 38-40.

[71] Strauss, *op. cit.,* 136-137; Palmer, *op. cit.,* 35; Pomfret, *op. cit.,* 44-46; Locker-Lampson, *op. cit.,* 265.

[72] Quoted from testimony of W. S. Trench in *Report from the Select Committee of the House of Lords on the Tenure (Ireland) Bill (H. L.); Together with the Proceedings of the Committee, Minutes of Evidence and Index* (H. C. 1867), 28.   Cited hereafter as *Report Select Committee House of Lords Tenure Ireland Act, 1867.*

[73] Locker-Lampson, *op. cit.,* 264-265; Strauss, *op. cit.,* 137; Palmer, *ibid.*

[74] *Report Select Committee House of Lords Tenure Ireland Act,* 1867, 252, 271; *Report Select Committee Tenure Ireland Act. 1865,* 106-107; Locker-Lampson, *ibid.;* King, *op. cit.,* 84; Bernard H. Becker, *Disturbed Ireland* (London, 1881), 215-224.

lightning rod for peasant discontent, drawing upon themselves the bolts of peasant wrath which might well have struck their superiors, the mushroom aristocrats laid open the entire landlord class to the bitter criticism of reformers and the fury of the dispossessed.[75] William O'Brien, passionate leader of the land wars in the National League days and lieutenant of Parnell, received his first adult impressions of Irish landlords from a miserably rack-rented estate which the encumbered estates courts had turned over to speculators. "From the knowledge then acquired," he later wrote, "I date that persuasion [of mine] that Landlordism is the deepest root of Irish misery . . . ."[76] His articles in the Dublin's *Freeman's Journal*, widely publicized in Ireland and America, persuaded others to the same conclusions.[77]

Though the Encumbered Estates Act failed to quiet Ireland, British politicians for many years retained their faith in the idea that Ireland's economic salvation lay in the large farm, run according to "those economical principles of free and open competition" that made England great, to quote an efficient if unpopular practitioner of these principles in Ireland.[78] The Deasy Act of 1860 declared tenant and landlord to have a purely contractual relationship; thus substituting free trade for feudal tenure, only to increase the power of the landlords, for sharp competition nullified the bargaining position of the tenant.[79]

Under the impact of agitation in Ireland and the teaching of

---

[75] Locker-Lampson, *op. cit.*, 264-265; Sarah L. Steele, *The Right Honorable Arthur MacMorrough Kavanagh* (London, 1891), minority report of Kavanagh as member of Bessborough Commission, Appendix E., 309. See also statistics showing direct relationship between agrarian crime and sales in encumbered estates courts, in *Irish Land Question as to Tenant Right.* (n.d., n.p.) 19-22, bound in *Report Select Committee Tenure Ireland Act, 1865;* Blunt, *op. cit.*, 112.

[76] William O'Brien, *op. cit.*, 188.

[77] William O'Brien, *op. cit.*, 188-197; *Irish World,* July 20, 1878. Another case given wide publicity was that of James Scully, former middleman, who purchased an estate at Ballycohey, Tipperary and from 1847 to 1868 fought a more or less continuous war with his tenants. Later he purchased land in America. *Irish World,* May. 18, 1878; Boston *Pilot,* April 3, 1886; Locker-Lampson, 337; Michael Davitt, *The Fall of Feudalism in Ireland* (London, 1904), 77.

[78] Jones, *op. cit.*, 146. For English attitudes toward Irish economic problems see George O'Brien, *op. cit.*, 582; Pomfret, *op. cit.*, chapters II and III.

[79] Pomfret, *op. cit.*, 46-49; Palmer, *op. cit.*, 36-37.

John Stuart Mill and others in England the House of Commons gradually shifted its position, recognizing that one did not legislate in the same way for a poor agricultural nation as for a rich industrial one.[80] In the Land Acts of 1870 and 1881 the legal machinery to protect the right of the tenant to the land he worked was fabricated and a start made toward peasant proprietorship. The stone of the landed aristocracy, mourned Standish O'Grady in 1882, "rolls irrecoverable to the abyss."[81]

His prophecy was, of course, accurate, but old habits were only slowly abandoned. In 1888 a Mayo landlord fined a tenant for marrying without consent,[82] and in that same year Michael Davitt, who perhaps did more than anyone else to start that stone rolling, angrily rebuked the tenantry of Earl Fitzgibbon for their anxiety to present that nobleman with a gift upon his golden wedding anniversary.[83]

The Famine served as the final pressure which fractured the casting of the old Irish social order. Along with the dwarf holdings, the cottier system was swept away in most of Leinster and Munster, when farmers and landlords, refusing or unable to support their pauper laborers, pushed them into the villages.[84] Thus alienated from the land, this rural proletariat offered a massive unrest to anyone bold enough to use them in recasting Irish society.[85]

Never firmly settled upon the backs of the people, the Irish gentry began to lose their grip when they resorted to the policy of eviction and consolidation. Though convinced that they were acting in the best interests of the nation, it could not be expected that the uprooted rural masses would share their conviction.

---

[80] Pomfret, *op. cit.*, 72-74; Palmer, *Ibid.*

[81] In Palmer, *op. cit.*, 256.

[82] Boston *Pilot*, June 23, 1888.

[83] William Henry Hurlbert, *Ireland Under Coercion* (Boston, 1888), IX.

[84] Strauss, *op. cit.*, 139; King, *op. cit.*, 269; Jones, *op. cit.*, 5-7, 10-11, and Kavanagh in Steele, *op. cit.*, 176-177 argue that the destruction of the potato and promise of poor relief brought the cottier into the village. Estate rules against the building of laborer's dwellings, however, kept him there.

[85] See Strauss, *op. cit.*, 139, 146; King, *op. cit.*, 274-276; John O'Leary, *Recollections of Fenians and Fenianism* (London, 1896), II, 143, 238; also letter of former Irish farm laborer bitterly critical of farmers in *Irish World*, April 2, 1881.

"Edged back upon a tract of clouds and obsession . . . ,"[86] the gentry lost touch with the people and stagnated. Political leadership passed into the hands of the aggressive Catholic middle-class who had been accumulating wealth since the Penal days.

There were, however, serious limitations upon the ability of the parvenue to assume authority. In a poor nation his rise to affluence was often accomplished at the expense of his neighbors. Dislike for him was increased by the eagerness with which he lusted after the petty honors and spoils of political office to the prejudice of his independence. The emancipated Catholic, said Gavan Duffy, was far too anxious to sit at the feasts of his former enemies.[87]

Towards a New Ireland

Under the pressure of the forces of change, a new order was emerging in Ireland. The formidable task faced by the Irish nationalist was how to mold its character, how to formulate political and social ideals meaningful to all regions of Ireland and all classes and kinds of Irishmen. Toward the accomplishment of this, the reformer had certain advantages.

There was first of all the Catholic church. Rooted deeply in the history of Ireland, endeared to the people by the common suffering of the Penal Days, only recently purged of abuses by prelates like the vigorous "JKL," James Doyle, Bishop of Kildare and Leighlin, the Church was prepared to serve the Irish people.[88] O'Connell erected his structure of agitation upon the shoulders of the parish priests and where their support was weak, as in Connemara before 1840, the movements were weak.[89]

The Irish hierarchy, however, was very conservative and cautious, especially so while the influence of the older continental trained clergy and the clerical refugees of the French Revolution

---

[86] Bowen, op. cit., 258.
[87] Duffy, Young Ireland, 11.
[88] See Fitzpatrick; Dr. Doyle, vol. I, 104-117 for reforms of Dr. Doyle.
[89] Not until 1840 did Archbishop McHale give permission to agitate for Repeal in his diocese of Tuam. See O'Connell's letter to McHale, July 30, 1840, in W. J. Fitzpatrick, The Correspondence of Daniel O'Connell, 2 vols. (Dublin, 1888), II, 246.

lasted.[90] Bishop Doyle, outspoken both in his loyalty to the British constitution and in his insistence that the Roman Catholics of Ireland be permitted to share in its privileges, was something of a shock to his colleagues.[91] O'Connell, for the most part, received support from the hierarchy in the agitation to repeal the Union, but Young Ireland was not so honored.[92]

When Thomas Davis, Protestant creator of the Young Ireland nationalists, assured the Irish people, in popular doggerel, that what mattered was their devotion to the Irish nation and not that "at different shrines we pray unto one God," he aroused suspicions that a Mazzini was abroad in Ireland.[93] The belief that Irish nationalism was cut from the same cloth as the atheistic nationalism of the continent, trickily manipulated by the enemies of Davis and his followers, cost them the support of the clergy and thus blocked one avenue of communication with the mass of the people. The Young Irelanders unwisely ignored the advice given them to "never butt your head against a wall—especially a church wall."[94]

Fear of Irish nationalism persisted in clerical thought. Bishop Cullen, Bishop of Armagh and Apostolic Delegate to Ireland at the time Gavan Duffy organized his Tenant Right League in the 1850's, "smelling Mazzini everywhere,"[95] exerted his influence over the clergy and the Catholic middle-class to smash that movement.[96] Not until the advent of Archbishop Walsh in 1885 could

---

[90] For viewpoints of the Irish clergy see C. G. Duffy, *The League of the North and the South* (London, 1886), 312-313; Lecky, *op. cit.*, III, 353-370; John O'Driscoll, *Views of Ireland*, 2 vols. (London, 1823), II, 111-118. Fitzpatrick, *Dr. Doyle*, I, 505-506; Wyse, *op. cit.*, I, 237-240.

[91] Fitzpatrick, *Dr. Doyle*, I, 93, 231, 351; II, 3, 81, 346-355.

[92] John F. Broderick, *The Holy See and the Irish Movement for the Repeal of the Union with England, 1829-1847.* Analecta Gregoriana, LV (Rome, 1951), 215-216, 226-228.

[93] Michael Tierney "Thomas Davis. 1814-1845," *Studies*, XXXIV (1945) 307, 309; Charles Gavan Duffy, *Four Years of Irish History* (London, 1883), 26, 330, 361, 445. John O'Leary accepted Davis' poem as expressing the spirit of Fenianism. O'Leary, *op. cit.*, II, 178. Ironically, some European liberals scorned Irish nationalism as priest ridden. See statement of Louis Blanc in Duffy, *Four Years*, 569; and "The Irish Difficulty, by a Foreign Liberal," *Frazer's Magazine*, n.s. XXVI, July 1882, 120-149.

[94] Duffy, *Four Years*, 330.

[95] Bowen, *op. cit.*, 354. 122; Thomas P. O'Connor, *The Irish Parliamentary Party* (London, 1886), 126 ff.

[96] Duffy, *League of North and South*, 300-381; Davitt, *op. cit.*, 70-71,

nationalists count upon support from the Archbishop of Dublin.[97] Walsh, however, along with Archbishop Croke, since youth a friend to land reform and nationalism, were under frequent fire from Rome, where Irish problems were necessarily related to the welfare of the entire Church. "I'm not only the Pope of Ireland, but of the Universal Church," Pope Leo XIII is reported to have said in 1883 to Archbishop Croke, whom the Vatican considered a kind of Irish Garibaldi, "and I can't sacrifice the Church to Ireland."

"No, nor Ireland to the Church," the Archbishop was said to have replied.[98]   Croke, however, did not, as this answer suggests, value nationalism above Catholicism; but he did realize the danger of alienating the Irish people by obstructing nationalists plans for land reform.[99]   When Parnell's sorry relationship with Mrs. O'Shea was made public, Croke joined with Walsh in proposing to the hierarchy the public condemnation which led to the Irish leader's tragic fall.[100]   Nationalists needed clerical support, but it was even a dangerous two-edged sword.[101]

"Educate that you may be free," taught Thomas Davis, who understood the value of education in expanding the horizons of the Irish people.[102]   In the eighteenth and first part of the nineteenth centuries Catholics, for the most part, had to be content with the instruction offered by the Hedge Schools. Held in a barn or hut, or beneath a hedge in summer, presided over by a seedy schoolmaster, jammed with ragged children, the schools at best offered a knowledge of the classics and sufficient mathematics to

---

[97] Philip Bagenal, *The Priest in Politics* (London, 1893), 1-17; also Duffy, *Ibid.*, 372, 377; Blunt, *op. cit.*, 43.   Davitt, *op. cit.*, 403, bitterly critical of Catholic Hierarchy, says only Archbishop Croke defended the Irish cause against Vatican charges.

[98] Told by Croke to Wilfrid Scawen Blunt, in Blunt, *op. cit.*, 280.   Davitt, *op. cit.*, 400 records conversation differently.

[99] William O'Brien, *op. cit.*, 281-282; Blunt, *op. cit.*, 98; For nationalist criticism of Croke in 1875, which may possibly have had bearing upon his attitude toward Land League, see *Irish World*, September 18, 1875, and October 9, 1875.

[100] William O'Brien, *op. cit.*, 282; F. S. L. Lyons, *The Irish Parliamentary Party, 1890-1910* (London, 1950), 27.

[101] For bitter criticism of papal policy in Ireland written by Irish-American follower of Henry George and typical of extreme nationalists, see J. G. Maguire, *Ireland and the Pope* (San Francisco, 1888).

[102] Thomas Davis, *Selections From His Prose and Poetry*, T. W. Rolleston, ed. Every Irishman's Library (London, 1914), 232.

figure out the rent due the landlords, and at the worst an unhappy experience with a brutal pedant.[103] Munster was tradi-
tionally the home of such schools, but they were plentiful elsewhere, with the exception perhaps of Connaught, where Bishop
Doyle in 1824 reported the people "buried in destitution, filth and
misery.[104]

Efforts to improve the education offered the masses of the
Irish were frustrated by sectarian quarrels over management of
the schools. When the Kildare Street schools, begun in 1811 and
subsidized by the government after 1815, became Protestant
proselytizing institutions, many Catholics withdrew.[105] The National School system, begun in 1833, was also badly mauled by
sectarianism. Accepted at first by the majority of the hierarchy
of the Catholic church, the National schools met with the formidable opposition of Archbishop McHale, who feared they would
follow the proselytizing path of the Kildare Street schools. "Better
enter Heaven possessed of no earthly learning, than to go to Hell
possessing the learning of a Socrates, an Aristotle or a Cicero,"
reasoned the Archbishop, according to his biographer.[106] The
same sentiment compelled him to oppose the establishment of the
Queen's Colleges ("the Godless colleges") in 1845 at Cork, Galway and Belfast.

Subsequent events seemed to confirm the suspicions of the
redoubtable John of Tuam and in 1869 the hierarchy, under the
leadership of Cardinal Cullen, condemned mixed education of
Protestant and Catholics on both the primary and college levels.[107]
As a consequence, National schools became increasingly denomi-

---

[103] See Carleton, *op. cit.*, "The Hedge School," II, 198-266 and the
"Poor Scholar," III, 179-307; Constantia Maxwell, *op. cit.*, 167-171. For
other early schools see Locker-Lampson, *op. cit.*, 125-138.

[104] Fitzpatrick, *Dr. Doyle*, vol. I, 177.

[105] Locker-Lampson, *op. cit.*, 139-140; Fitzpatrick, *Dr. Doyle*, I, 323-324.

[106] Ulick Bourke, *The Life and Times of the Most Reverend John
McHale* (New York, 1883), 108. For McHale's fight against the National
School system and the Queens Colleges see *ibid.*, 103-110; O'Faolain, *op. cit.*,
268-269; Locker-Lampson, *op. cit.*, 142-144, 349-354; L. Paul-Dubois, *op. cit.*,
485-486.

[107] Bourke, *op. cit.*, 106. The Queen's Colleges were condemned by the
Synod of Thurles in 1850 and sons of Catholic parents warned not to enter
them. *Ibid.*, 156. Also Locker-Lampson, *op. cit.*, 353 and L. Paul-Dubois,
op. cit., 486.

national. In 1880 there were 669,595 Catholics out of a total of
699,199 pupils enrolled in the National schools of Leinster, Munster and Connacht. The total number of schools with a mixed attendance under Catholic management was 1,867. Only 43 schools
had both a mixed staff and mixed attendance.[108] By the end of
the century mixed National schools were comparatively rare and
the ban on the Queens Colleges was continued.[109]

Although the National schools failed to lessen sectarian ani-
mosities and their curricula was designed to inculcate loyalty to
England, they nevertheless served the cause of Irish nationalism
by increasing the literacy of the Irish people, enabling them to
comprehend nationalist propaganda.[110] In 1841 72 percent of
the people of the four provinces were unable to read and write;
52 percent were unable to read *or* write. By 1871 these figures
had been lowered by twenty percentage points and the hopes of
Davis partially realized.[111]

Increased skill in the use of English was obtained, of course,
at the expense of Gaelic.[112] The Irish language, however much
an article of faith for modern nationalists, was not of primary
interest to nationalists throughout most of the nineteenth century.[113] And the decline in the use of Gaelic began long before
the National schools. The custom in these schools of punishing
pupils who clung to the Gaelic was done after all with the cooperation of the parents and appears also to have been practiced

---

[108] Locker-Lampson, *op. cit.*, 145.

[109] Locker-Lampson, *op. cit.*, 147; King, *op. cit.*, 289-290; L. Paul-Dubois,
op. cit., 370.

[110] Newspapers were undoubtedly the most important medium of nationalists propaganda. See King, *op. cit.*, 293; Palmer, *op. cit.*, 120 ff.; William
O'Brien, *op. cit.*, 273-274.

[111] King, *op. cit.*, 290; Pym, *op. cit.*, 306.

[112] In 1841 there were 1,204,684 persons who spoke both Irish and
English and 319,602 who spoke Irish only; in 1871 there were 714,313 who
spoke both languages and 102,562 who spoke Irish only. King, *op. cit.*,
293-294. In 1901 only 20,953 spoke Irish only. L. Paul-Dubois, *op. cit.*, 394.

[113] Among the Young Irelanders only Thomas Davis, John Mitchel and
Smith O'Brien were interested. Duffy, *Young Ireland*, 561-562. The Fenians
included a number of native speakers, among whom O'Donovan Rossa was most
interested in the language. O'Donovan Rossa, *Rossa's Recollections* (Mariner's
Harbor, N. Y., 1898), 80, 172, 177. Some slight interest was shown by
members of Parnell's Parliamentary party. T. M. Healy, *Letters and Leaders
of My Day*. 2 vols. (New York, 1929), I, 182-185. For language movement
see Desmond Ryan, *The Sword of Light* (London, 1939).

in the old Hedge schools.[114] The realistic Irish peasant abandoned his native language simply because it would not "sell the cow."[115]

Nor is it likely that Gaelic would have "sold" the ideals of nationalism to the people, for the songs and poems which kept nationalism alive in Dublin and New York (whether "The Wearing of the Green" or Kathleen ni Houlihan) were English in mood, as well as in words, and "utterly alien from the thought and spirit of Irish-speaking Ireland."[116]

More accurately, the mood was European and the National Schools and Queens Colleges, however anti-Irish, spawned nationalists because they brought the student into contact with European thought.[117] The Cork Queens College, "like all the rest of the elaborate plans for de-Catholicizing and denationalizing Ireland," writes William O'Brien, "gave England no better return for her pieces of silver than Balaam made to Balak when he was sent for to curse Israel."[118] Light from the fires of Europe, which the schools could not help but admit, illuminated not only the fallen state of the Irish nation, but the path which Europe suggested led to national salvation.

The peasant's hatred for English rule, reported by many observers and recorded in song and story, offered obvious advantages to the nationalist.[119] Yet, as Lecky suggests, the antipathy of the peasant was often superficial and sentimental.[120] The English

---

[114] L. Paul-Dubois, *op. cit.*, 394 and Mark Ryan, *op. cit.*, 8 describe the manner of punishment. Bourke, *op. cit.*, 32-33 reveals the similar methods used in Connaught in the late eighteenth century.

[115] Murphy, *op. cit.*, 5; John M. Synge, *In Wicklow and West Kerry* (Dublin, 1921), 63.

[116] Donal O'Sullivan, "Some Aspects of Irish Music and Poetry," *The Journal of the Royal Society of Antiquaries of Ireland.* Vol. LXXIX, (1949), 97. See also Michael Tierney, "Repeal of the Union," in *Nine Centenary Essays,* 151..

[117] See Michael Tierney, "Thomas Davis: 1814-1845," and "Nationalism: Survey," *Studies,* XXXIV, (1945), 300-310 and 474-482 for suggestive discussions of European roots fo Irish nationalism.

[118] William O'Brien, *op. cit.*, 163. He found a revolutionary circle at Cork College, and John O'Leary found followers of Davis at the Galway College. O'Leary, *op. cit.*, 50. Mark F. Ryan, another Fenian also studied at Galway. Ryan, *op. cit.*, Introduction.

[119] Constantia Maxwell, *op. cit.*, 72; Inglis, *op. cit.*, 210; *Sportsman in Ireland,* I, 77-78. Thomas Crofton Croker, *Researches in the South of Ireland* (London, 1824), 14.

[120] Lecky, *op. cit.*, IV, 2. Constantia Maxwell, *op. cit.*, 183.

traveller who found hatred for England among the peasantry experienced little dislike for Englishmen, who could travel into the most remote districts and find in some hut a generous and hospitable welcome.[121]

It would perhaps be more accurate to describe the peasant's attitude as rhetorical, as conforming to a literary tradition rather than to experience. For the peasant who sang songs thick with bitterness against the brutal Protestant Sassenach might never have experienced personally that species of tyrant.[122] His immediate oppressors would more likely be from his own kind—the small farmer who screwed up the price of rents or screwed down the price of labor, the estate bailiff or the usurious Gombeenman —peasants anxiously climbing out of poverty over the bodies of their fellows.[123]

Many of the songs of the Gaelic peasant derived indirectly from the culture of the ancient bardic order.[124] Professionally attached to their aristocratic patrons, whether Saxon or Gael, the bards were ruined in the Stuart wars of the seventeenth century. In the following century, the successors to the bards, indistinguishable in their poverty from the peasantry, enshrined the hopes and ideals of the fallen aristocrats in the Aisling or vision poem. The vision which comes to the Aisling poet while asleep, weary from lamenting the sorrows of the Gael, is that of Ireland, resplendent as a beautiful woman who prophecies the return of the Stuart and the restoration of the Gael.[125]

To recall vanished glories in the Aisling must have been a necessary narcotic for Irishmen reduced to beggary on lands once theirs. But they were comparatively few. A great many of the gentry fled after the Wild Geese,[126] to serve in the courts and armies of Europe; while others, like the O'Connells of Derrynane, carved out a place for themselves within the Penal code, held on

---

[121] Inglis, op. cit., 58: Sportsman, I. 152.
[122] Sportsman in Ireland, I, 122, 143; Report House of Lords Tenure Act, 1867, 155; Corkery, op. cit., 24.
[123] Corkery, ibid.; Jones, op. cit., O'Leary, op. cit., II, 44, 143. On extortions of Gombeenman see Report on Manor Courts in Ireland, 53; Becker, op. cit., 207 ff.
[124] Corkery, op. cit., 59-89; O'Sullivan, op. cit., 93-95.
[125] Corkery, op. cit., 128-130; O'Sullivan, op. cit., 97.
[126] Lecky, op. cit., I, 244. 248-251; George O'Brien, The Economic History of Ireland in the Seventeenth Century (London 1919), 214.

there tenaciously, and when Emancipation came emerged wealthy and loyal to the government.[127]

For the peasantry illusions of ancient grandeur may have served, as Sean O'Faolain suggests, to "distract the hovels from their misery, and to keep . . . their native pride alive;"[128] but they had little meaning for their immediate lives, or even for the lives of their forbears. When the French invasion fleet anchored in 1796 in Bantry, whose waters lap the shore of intensely Gaelic Kerry, the peasantry remained conspicuously quiet,[129] despite the traditions of hostility to the Hanoverians and the information they must have had of the ferment of freedom stirring on the continent.

The songs circulated during the tense years when the Revolution of 1798 was simmering and the French landing awaited were often truncated adaptations of the Aisling, with the French or "Boney" in place of the Stuarts as "deliverers."[130] In some of the songs there is a curious union of the Jacobite with the Jacobin; modern symbols evoking the seventeenth century aspirations of Sarsfield and the Wild Geese.[131] Neither the promise of a demo-

> Strong and valiant will we be;
> In Castlebar is Bonaparte
> Demanding Sarsfield's law.

cratic future, however, nor nostalgia for an aristocratic past were sufficient to arouse the peasantry.

Hope for relief from the desperate conditions of rural life brought many of the peasants into the United Irishmen movement and fear of Orange terrorism drove a minority of them into a violent if shortlived revolt in 1798.[132] To the democratic

---

[127] Gwynn, op. cit., 15-25, 154; O'Faolain, op. cit., 41-51; Murphy, op. cit., 19.

[128] O'Faolain, op. cit., 36. Croker, Researches in the South of Ireland, 225 describes impoverished peasants who boast of their honorable ancestry and speak of drawing rooms in their mud cabins. See G. O'Brien, ibid., 33-36.

[129] Lecky, op. cit., III, 540-543; Locker-Lampson, op. cit., 50. Communication with the continent was had through the Catholic gentry and smugglers. See Corkery, op. cit., 54 and Lecky, op. cit., III, 224.

[130] Murphy, op. cit., 19-20..

[131] See Richard Hayes, The Last Invasion of Ireland. 2nd Edition. (Dublin, 1939), 245 for following translation of Irish song contemporary with the landings at Killala. "The French are in Killala,

[132] Lecky, op. cit., III, 385-388, 412-414; IV, 267, 288-291; R. B. McDowell, Irish Public Opinion: 1750-1800 (London, 1943), 215; Locker-Lampson, op. cit., 51-54.

dogma of the United Irishmen the peasantry were indifferent and perhaps hostile.[133] The French, taught to believe in the general disaffection of the Irish masses from the government, were disappointed with the numbers who joined them after the landings at Killala.[134] To the peasant the game could not have been worth the candle, for the French and their allies among the Irish gentry took immediate steps to preserve private property and the status quo.[135] Like many Irish nationalists of later years, the French failed to understand that the peasant's hatred of England, however real as a rhetorical tradition, did not touch the heart of his anxieties, which were rooted in the land. Although an English traveller could move unmolested in Ireland, the rackrenter, whether English or Irish, Catholic or Protestant, was ever in danger.

The greatest foes to English law in Ireland, and great potential allies of Irish nationalism once properly understood, were the secret societies the peasants formed to resist the pressure of the rackrent—symbol for all those forces which mired the peasant in poverty and which threatened to drive him from the land. It was not, however, simply the experience of unchanging squalor, which induced a contentment of its own,[136] that drove the peasant to revolt, but rather the tightening of the screw of the rack. The rich counties of the midlands and the Southeast, not the barren West, spawned the most numerous secret societies.[137] The Whiteboy first appeared in Munster in 1761 when the waste-

---

[133] John O'Driscoll, *Views of Ireland, Moral, Political and Religious.* 2 vols. (London, 1823), II, 205-6; Lecky, *op. cit.,* IV, 291.

[134] Hayes, *op. cit.,* 58, 87-88.

[135] *Ibid.,* 59, 66-67. Hayes believes the Irish failed to rally around because they felt the position of the French hopeless and feared reprisals. Elsewhere, however, brutality of the government forces stimulated revolt. *Supra,* 30 and T. A. Emmet's examination before Secret Committee of House of Lords, 1798 in Richard R. Madden, *The United Irishmen, Their Lives and Times,* Third Series, Second Ed., (Lond. 1860), Vol. III, 65.

[136] Constantia Maxwell, *op. cit.,* 151-153; *Sportsman in Ireland,* I 144; Lewis, *op. cit.,* 88-90.

[137] Tipperary was usually the most "disturbed" county. Lewis, *op. cit.,* 43-44; *Devon Commission,* I, 331. See *Land (Ireland) Confidential* bound in *Report Select Committee Tenure Ireland Act, 1865;* for most disturbed counties, 1849-1869: Tipperary, Leitrim, King's, Longford, Westmeath. Then Clare, Queen's, Limerick, Meath, Kilkenny, Wexford, Louth and Wicklow.

lands, upon which his cattle grazed or pigs rooted, were enclosed. The Hearts of Steel boys terrorized Antrim in the early 1770's when Lord Donegal raised the rents and his agent demanded extortionate fines for the renewal of leases.[138] As the conditions of rural life worsened in the years between the Treaty of Vienna and the Famine secret societies proliferated. Many of their leaders had been "strong farmers" during the prosperous years of the Napoleonic wars who had lost their holdings in the depression which followed.[139]

Drawing most of their members from impoverished cottiers, farmers' sons, whom the movement against subdivision would leave landless, and unmarried servants, the societies used the tactics of terrorism to control the letting of land and the wages of labor.[140] They virtually established a state within a state. "A complete system of legislation," reported Wellesley, Lord Lieutenant of Ireland in 1834 to Melbourne, "with the most prompt, vigorous, and severe executive power, sworn, equipped, and armed for all purposes of savage punishment, is established in almost every district."[141]

Legislation was simple and the punishment cruel. A farmer who employed a laborer from outside the district would be directed by night visitors to discharge him. If this was refused a bit of burning turf might be thrust into the thatch of the farmer's cottage, or he might be seriously beaten. Retaliation against an estate that kept grazing lands out of tillage might be to cut off the tails of the cattle or otherwise maim them; or, as the Terry Alts did in Clare in 1832, spade up the grass land so that it had to be let for potatoes.[142] The deadly sin was to take land over the head of another. Violence trailed eviction notices like a tiger and the peasant who took over a holding from which a fellow had been ejected did so in peril of his life. The Irish peasant, said John Stuart Mill, "has nothing to hope and nothing

[138] For origin of various peasant societies see Lewis, op. cit., 4-35; Constantia Maxwell, op. cit., 173-174; Locker-Lampson, op. cit., 18-22.

[139] Testimony in Lewis, op. cit., 73-74.

[140] Lewis, op. cit., 99-102; Devon Commission, I, 321.

[141] Quoted in Lewis, op. cit., 100.

[142] Lewis, op. cit., 108-109, 184, 201, 226; Devon Commission, 321, 336. 321, 336.

to fear, except being dispossessed of his holding, and against this he defends himself by the *ultima ratio* of a defensive war."[143]

The agrarian wars, as O'Connell noted, pitted the poor against the poor.[144] The peasant, who saw directly, struck at the nearest oppressors, the tithe proctor, the bailif, the hard farmer—those whose ambitions drove them to violate the code of their class and whose punishment brought immediate relief.[145] The "squireens" serving as middlemen or agents, though thoroughly detested, were less vulnerable to attack because of their firearms and strong stone houses. To strike at them also entailed greater risks because they were not bound by the code which imposed silence upon the victims, while offering the prestige of Synge's Playboy to its executors.[146]

The same factors protected the landlords. Moreover, so long as faith in the gentry as protectors of the poor survived, they escaped the blows which fell upon their underlings. In Kildare in 1832 terrorists warned the farmers "to return their undertenants to the head landlord, at the same rates . . . for which they hold themselves. And we trust the gentlemen will not allow them to tyrannize over the impoverished poor of this nation."[147]

After the 1830's members of secret agrarian societies increasingly came to be called Ribbonmen, but they retained their old Whiteboy character. Their violence was invariably motivated by specific loyal grievances connected with the land;[148] that of the Ribbonmen proper derived from religious hostility, whether in town or country, and was to be found largely in the North and wherever else Catholic and Protestant populations were sufficient-

---

[143] Quoted by John Blake Dillon in *Report House of Lords Tenure Ireland Act, 1867*, 112. Also Lewis, *op. cit.*, 61, 80; *Devon Commission*, I, 321. See statistics showing relationship between evictions and crime in *Land (Ireland)*, 18-19.

[144] O'Faolain, *op. cit.*, 261; Lewis, *op. cit.*, 239.

[145] Lewis, *op. cit.*, 48, 53, 67. 238-9; *Devon Commission*, I, 320.

[146] Inglis, *op. cit.*, 197; Steele, *op. cit.*, 253-254; E. Cant-Wall, *Ireland Under the Land Act* (London, 1882), 157.

[147] In Lewis, *op. cit.*, 221. For similar expressions see *Devon Commission*, I, 332 and testimony of Bishop Keane in *Report Select Committee Tenure Ireland Act., 1865*, 189.

[148] Best discussion of this matter is to be found in Leahy, *op. cit.*, where testimony of Thomas Drummond and other informed persons supports this view. See especially pp. 60, 66-67, 72. See also Lewis, *op. cit.*, 156 ff. for similar testimony from Daniel O'Connell and others.

ly large and in . close enough contact to generate friction.[149]
Where religious discrimination against Catholics was sometimes a
factor in the letting of land, as in Antrim and Armagh, Ribbonism and Whiteboyism would be indistinguishable.[150]

Elsewhere, agrarian combinations sometimes used Ribbon
oaths; but these, whether innocuous declarations of brotherhood
and loyalty to the king, or vows to "Cut Down Kings, Queens and
Princes, Dukes, Earls, Lords and all such with Land Jobin and
Herrisy," did not determine the behavior of the members, and
were irrelevant to their main concern.[151] In seeking redress of
their grievances, the peasants were non-sectarian. "The White-
feet are most liberal people," testified a parish priest in 1832,
"for they make no distinction between Catholic and Protestant."[152]   Their liberalism had been demonstrated in the previous year when a brother of the Catholic Bishop of Kilkenny
had been murdered for speculating in land.[153] Neither were they
interested in radical political solutions of Ireland's problems. It
was easier in 1848 and 1867, said John O'Leary, "to make a
rebel out of an Orangeman than of a Ribbonman."[154]

Like the Luddites of England who smashed the machinery
threatening their handloom economy, the Whiteboys were lawless
and violent; yet not without reason, for "hunger will break
through stone walls,"[155] and not without purpose. Whiteboyism
(or Ribbonism) played a not inconsiderable part in breaking
down the parochialism of Irish life. Feudal ties and factions

---

[149] Leahy, *op. cit.*, 50; Inglis, *op. cit.*, 270; Beaumont, *op. cit.*, II,
15. Davitt, *op. cit.*, 41-43, believes Ribbon combination absorbed Whiteboyism after 1830, but he limits Ribbon influence to Ulster and the counties
stretching from Louth westward to the northern counties of Connacht.

[150] See *Devon Commission* testimony quoted in *Reports of the Parliamentary Committee of the Royal National Repeal Association of Ireland* (Dublin,
1845), II, lxxvii; lxxxix, xcii.

[151] Lewis, *op. cit.*, 167. The oaths vary greatly in character. For others
markedly loyal and mild see Leahy, *op. cit.*, 61-65.

[152] In Lewis, *op. cit.*, 131. See also *ibid.*, 125-136; Leahy, *op. cit.*, 4,
10-11; Blunt, *op. cit.*, 47-48.

[153] Lewis, *op. cit.*, 115-116; Davitt, *op. cit.*, 39.

[154] O'Leary, *op. cit.*, 111. Davitt, however, whose life was dedicated to
bringing the national and agrarian movements together, says Ribbon society
exercised "very considerable influence" upon Fenian brotherhood. Davitt,
op. cit., 41. See Strauss, *op. cit.*, 145-147.

[155] Duffy, *League of North and South*, 17.

tended to dissolve in the common fight for the land.[156] Although it is not true that a national peasant underground was formed, bound together by Ribbon oaths and passwords, there was co-operation among embattled neighboring districts in providing night raiders and in protecting them from the law.[157] Understanding of the desperate need for holding on to the land was common among all the small occupiers and "without any expressed agreement, was well calculated to produce among them that uniformity of action, which is found to prevail in Ireland, in resisting the exercise of legal rights."[158]

However merciless their methods and illusory their hopes, the Whiteboys served the cause of the agrarian poor[159] and served also to demonstrate in a terrible way the inadequacies of British rule in Ireland.[160]

Two Possibilities

In 1828 when the forty-shilling freeholders of County Clare, rebelling against their landlords, elected Daniel O'Connell to the British Parliament, despite the fact that as a Catholic that honor was barred to him, they tugged loose one of the necessary props of feudal Ireland. Sir Robert Peel, an old Irish hand, later stated that O'Connell's victory was "manifest proof that the sense of common grievance and the sympathies of common interest were beginning to loosen the ties which connect different classes of men in friendly relations to each other—to weaken the force of local and personal attachment, and to unite scattered elements of society into a homogeneous and disciplined mass . . . ."[161] The Irish people in 1828 were entering the modern world and for this O'Connell had been working for a quarter of a century.

From Kerry in the heart of Gaelic Ireland, O'Connell pos-

---

[156] See Edgeworth, *Tour in Connemara*, 64-65; Lewis, *op. cit.*, 290, 295; Davitt, *op. cit.*, 37.
[157] Lewis, *op. cit.*, 223; Leahy, *op. cit.*, 60; *supra*, 33.
[158] *Devon Commission*, I, 321.
[159] Pomfret, *op. cit.*, 25; Davitt, *op. cit.*, 77.
[160] Davitt, *op. cit.*, 100-103; Duffy, *League of North and South*, 17-19.
[161] Fitzpatrick, *Dr. Doyle*, II, 76. For O'Connell's work in bringing factions together in friendship see *Diary of Humphrey O'Sullivan*, part II, 19, 25-27. Also Wyse, *op. cit.*, I, 206-207.

sessed the peasant's toughness and shrewdness and their love of words as well. In the phrase of Balzac, he was "the incarnation of a people,"[162] but he had a self-discipline, which the peasantry lacked and ideas which were not theirs. He would leave the past, to lead Ireland into modernity, where the Hanoverians rather than the Stuarts ruled, and where the radical reforms of Jeremy Bentham suggested the way to achieve justice and good government for Ireland.[163]

O'Connell's achievements have frequently been disparaged, and only in our own day has his work been properly evaluated.[164] By his leadership and agitation he taught the Catholic people of Ireland the value of pride and even of arrogance, encouraging them to abandon the craven slouch of Penal times, and to combine in order to gain for themselves political power and social reform. In doing so he exerted a profound influence upon the "rise of a Catholic democratic movement all over the Continent."[165]

Peel's understanding of O'Connell as a powerful force in breaking down traditional social ties was perceptive, but it would not be true to say that the Liberator offered the mystique of modern nationalism as a substitute. It is true that both early and late in his career he demanded repeal of the Act of Union; not, however, because of any doctrinaire belief in Ireland's right to nationality, but because the "benefits of good government had not reached the great mass of the Irish people, and could not reach them unless the Union should be made either a *reality,* or unless that hideous measure should be abrogated."[166] When he was at the height of his Parliamentary power in 1835 he abandoned agitation for Repeal and supported the Whig government of Lord Melbourne. "There is but one magic in politics and that is, *to be always right* . . . let us honestly and sincerely test the

---

[162] In Gwynn, *op. cit.,* 2.

[163] See the essays of Murphy and Tierney in Tierney, *Centenary Essays.*

[164] See the brilliant first chapter of Sean O'Faolain's, *King of the Beggars.* Gwynn, in the introduction to his life of O'Connell, offers a good summary of the work of O'Connell's Irish detractors.

[165] Gwynn, *op. cit.,* 3.

[166] Ltr. to Earl of Shrewsbury, 1842; Fitzpatrick, *O'Connell Correspondence,* II, 285. See also Tierney, *Centenary Essays,* 158-160, 168.

Union in the hands of a friendly administration," he advised
disappointed Dubliners at the time, ". . . let us give them a clear
stage and all possible favour, to work the Union machinery for
the benefit of old Ireland."[167]

The test did not work. From Dublin Castle, under the guidance of Thomas Drummond, Ireland received decent treatment,
but the opposition of Peel, backed by the House of Lords, made
far-reaching legislative reforms impossible, so in 1838 O'Connell
founded his Precursor society. " 'The Precursors' may precede
justice to Ireland from the United Parliament and the consequent
dispensing with Repeal agitation. It may precede Repeal agitation—and will, shall, and must precede Repeal agitation if justice be refused," he wrote to a friend in 1838 in explanation of
the curious name he had chosen.[168]

By 1840 it was clear that reforms were not forthcoming, and
the Repeal society was then founded. To its cause O'Connell was
faithful until he died, with only brief deviation after his imprisonment in 1844.[169] For, as he wrote to a friend in 1846, the year
before he left for Genoa and death, the "English Parliament does
not dream of converting the Parchment Union into the semblance
of a real union by giving to the Irish nation equal franchises,
equal representation, equal rights, equal religious freedom—in
short equal laws with those enjoyed by the people of England."[170]

Lord Monteagle, a stout and consistent opponent of the Liberator, who called him "Mountgoose," thought that he used
"Repeal as a householder might use a wolf-dog in a leash, not
wishing to loose the animal, but to frighten those whom he considered as evil-doers with his howl."[171]   Monteagle was perhaps
thinking of the turbulent year of 1843 when O'Connell assembled
the people by the hundred-thousands in "monster meetings" to
exact repeal by the threat of overwhelming moral force, only to
retreat before the government when it countered with a more

---

[167] Fitzpatrick, *O'Connell Correspondence*, II, 7.
[168] Letter to P. V. Fitzpatrick, October 28, 1838, *ibid.*, 158.
[169] The plan for Federation, based on a Whig alliance. See Gavan Duffy,
Young Ireland, 575-609; Fitzpatrick, *O'Connell Correspondence*, II, 307-310.
[170] Letter to Martin Crean, February 13, 1846; Fitzpatrick, *O'Connell
Correspondence*, II, 367.
[171] *Ibid.*, I, 427-428 footnote.

impressive threat of physical force. The "wolf dog" was kept in leash that year only because O'Connell feared violent revolution, like so many of his generation who remembered the bloody knife of the guillotine.

His radicalism derived from England, not France; and being a Christian radicalism, peaceful agitation, not violence was its proper instrument.[172] The mystical belief of Mitchel and Pearse that the spilling of blood was necessary for Ireland's redemption would probably have been considered mischievous nonsense by the eminently practical O'Connell, for whom "one living Repealer was worth a churchyard full of dead ones."[173] Infrequently, perhaps by design, perhaps caught up in the rhythm of his own rhetoric, he uttered threats of violence in his public speeches, but these he hastily repudiated.[174]

O'Connell permitted no doubt about his loyalty to the Crown. For Victoria—"our young and lovely Queen"[175]—he had an old man's sentimental attachment. When George IV visited Ireland in 1821 the agitator outdid himself in paying court to the jaded monarch, much to the disgust of Lord Byron and to future generations of Irish nationalists. However, obsequiously expressed, O'Connell's loyalty to the Sovereign was in keeping with his political ambition to obtain for Ireland a status equal to that of England under the British constitution.

Although he was not above smiting the "Saxon" verbally, the great Dan was too much the cosmopolite to be exclusively and narrowly Irish. He conceived of his Repeal Association as seeking not only justice for Ireland, but reform for England as well.[176] His sympathy for the negro slave of America embarrassed the nationalists in the Repeal movement in 1845 and alienated the

---

[172] Tierney, *Centenary Essays*, 155-156. On origins of O'Connell's ideas see Gwynn, *op. cit.*, 44-48; O'Faolain, *op. cit.*, 73-78.

[173] Gwynn, *op. cit.*, 232; Tierney, *op. cit.*, 155; Fitzpatrick, *Correspondence of O'Connell*, II, Appendix, 436.

[174] Gwynn, *op. cit.*, 152-153, 232; Duffy, *Young Ireland*, 366.

[175] Fitzpatrick, *O'Connell Correspondence*, II, 102, from a speech in Bandon, Co. Cork. See also Gwynn, *op. cit.*, 227.

[176] Fitzpatrick, *O'Connell Correspondence*, II, letter to P. V. Fitzpatrick, April 9, 1940, 238.

Irish-Americans.[177] Interested, as Arthur Griffith suggested,[178] in achieving progress through the assimilation of English ways, he deeply resented the remark of Lord Lyndhurst that the Irish were "aliens in blood, in religion and in language";[179] and in maturity he abandoned the Irish tongue familiar to him from childhood and was, as he said, "sufficiently utilitarian" not to regret its passing.[180]

To the peasant, subject to the vagaries of nature, life was filled with mystery. If the cow failed to give milk, it was the work of the fairies. If the potato crop failed and starvation threatened, it was the will of God.[181] This fatalism enabled the people to face life with cheer and death with dignity, but it was not the attitude upon which an aggressive political order could be built. Without doubt O'Connell was of great influence in teaching the peasantry to relate their miseries to the British Parliament rather than exclusively to the inscrutable will of God.[182]

Nevertheless, it is difficult to determine how far from Dublin his ideas radiated and how deeply they penetrated the minds of the peasantry. Michael Doheny, on the run in 1848, came upon areas in Cork and Kerry where O'Connell was virtually unknown[183] and Thomas D'Arcy McGee had a similar experience in Leitrim and Sligo.[184] Archbishop McHale blocked off Connacht from the agitator until the 1840's and apparently his influence never became great there. Mark Ryan, the Fenian, said that during his youth in County Galway in the 1850's "The people knew nothing about the history of their country and the idea of an independent country was something beyond their wildest dreams."[185]

---

[177] See Handlin, *op. cit.*, 136; Duffy, *Young Ireland*, 745-749; Fitzpatrick, *O'Connell Correspondence*, II, 207-210, 349-350.

[178] Arthur Griffith, *Thomas Davin, The Thinker and Teacher* (Dublin, 1916), XII.

[179] Fitzpatrick, *O'Connell Correspondence*, II, 57, 363-364 and letter to P. V. Fitzpatrick, May 1839, II, 177-178.

[180] In Murphy, *op. cit.*, 4.

[181] Nicholson, *op. cit.*, 16, 109; *Diary of Humphrey O'Sullivan*, part III, 237; Rossa, *op. cit.*, 59-60, 110. For good description of peasant's reaction to famine see William Carleton's *The Black Prophet*.

[182] See Wyse, *op. cit.*, I, 210.

[183] Michael Doheny, *The Felon's Track* (Dublin, 1918), 250.

[184] "Thomas D'Arcy McGee's Narrative of 1848" in *ibid.*, 294.

[185] Ryan, *op. cit.*, 5.

The towns were the chief support of the Catholic Association. The country parishes, according to the historian of the Association, "continued more or less inert."[186] The towns were also the chief support of the Repeal Association. Repeal Association libraries were established in towns radiating out from Dublin, in the valley of the Shannon and the valleys of the eastern parts of the counties of Cork, Waterford and Kilkenny and as far north as Newry and Armagh.[187] Stocked with Irish histories and nationalist periodicals, the libraries offered patriotism as a substitute for whiskey which many an Irishman had forsworn by taking Father Matthew's temperance pledge. For most, however, the reading-room literature must have been a dull replacement for the gregarious excitement of the public house.

Aware that Catholic Emancipation had little appeal as such for the peasant, the Catholic Association tried to persuade him that it was not by "burnings or assassinations, or acts of local and immediate revenge, he could hope for redress,—it was by the removal of that principle of [religious] inequality, which was the fertile source from which every injury and provocation had flowed."[188] To demonstrate their point, they set up people's courts to offer "instant protection against local wrong," in contrast with the "slovenly and reluctant justice of his Majesty."[189]

The hopes of the peasantry were in that way stirred and when the act of Emancipation was passed bonfires sparked on the hills of Ireland. "They thought O'Connell and Shiel would stream gold in their pockets,"[190] but the only immediate effect of the act upon the peasantry was to disenfranchise some two hundred thousand of them.[191] And they were very bitter. "What good did the emancipation do us?" a parish priest reported the cottiers

[186] Wyse, op. cit., I, 209.
[187] Reports Parliamentary Committee of Repeal Association, II, 329-347. By April 1845, 85 "official" Reading Rooms were reported established.
[188] Wyse, op. cit., I, 299. See also testimony of T. A. Emmet and W. J. MacNeven on peasant and Catholic emancipation before the Secret Committee of the House of Lords, 1798 in Madden, op. cit., III, 66, 223-224, 227.
[189] Wyse, Ibid., 205.
[190] Mr. Gregory's Letter Box, ed. by Lady Gregory (1898), 267 in Strauss, op. cit., 99.
[191] Strauss, Ibid.

as complaining in 1832. "Are we better clothed or fed, or our children better clothed and fed? Are we not as naked as we were, and eating dry potatoes when we can get them? Let us notice the farmers to give us better food and better wages, and not give so much to the landlord and more to the workmen; we must not let them be turning the poor people off the ground."[192]

While O'Connell in 1832 was talking about Repeal, the people were turning toward Whiteboyism and rural Ireland was aflame with agrarian revolt. To ease the tension Repeal was dropped and the fight against the payment of tithes to the Established Church was taken up.[193] As a result the tithe was transformed in effect into a rent charge and the agrarian masses suffered disillusionment again. Nor is this surprising, for O'Connell met the unique problems of the poor only with the prejudices of his class.[194] He fought the Dublin trade unions and he fought their rural counterpart, the Whiteboys, and the "villanous miscreants,"[195] as he called the latter, fought back. At times they harrassed the notorious rackrenters among his followers,[196] as well as members of his Repeal Association.[197] And in 1831 and 1834 his political opponents made use of the Tammany tactics of the Terry Alts to embarrass his party at the polls.[198] Like Bishop Doyle, whose failure to control the secret organizations of his diocese almost drove him to despair,[199] O'Connell was never able to uproot the peasant societies. They were embedded too deeply in the potato culture of Ireland.

The "Monster Meetings" of 1843 offer the best evidence of O'Connell's popularity with the Irish people. Whatever part imagination played in compiling the statistics of attendance—the Repealers claimed that 400,000 met at Tara and the *Times* made

---

[192] In Lewis, *op. cit.*, 109.

[193] Strauss, *op. cit.*, 100-101. Testimony in Lewis, *op. cit.*, 120-122 suggests that the war of 1831-32 was not a Whiteboy concern and testimony on pages 174-178 that it resulted from O'Connell's agitation.

[194] Jesse D. Clankson, *Labour and Nationalism in Ireland* (New York, 1925), 133-136.

[195] Fitzpatrick, *O'Connell Correspondence*, I, 336-337, 263, 317.

[196] Lewis, *op. cit.*, 176.

[197] *Reported Parliamentary Committee Repeal Association*, II, 340, 345.

[198] Fitzpatrick, *O'Connell Correspondence*, I, 263, 493-494.

[199] Fitzpatrick, *Dr. Doyle*, II, 458.

it an even million—there is no doubt but that the crowds were immense.[200] But what meaning the meetings had for the people is not so obvious. O'Connell perhaps knew best when he refused to permit the people to assemble at the last great meeting at Clontarf in the face of opposition from the Queen's troops. Michael Doheny and Thomas Meagher harrangued a crowd reported at 50,000 in July of 1848 on the slopes of Slievenamon, which looks down upon the town of Ballingarry, where in a few weeks time their hopes for a successful revolution were to die for lack of support.[201] Perhaps some of those who came to hear the Liberator in 1843 were like that senile priest whose presence among the insurgents in 1848 heartened them until they learned that he later marched with the constabulary and was after all only out to see the show.[202]

To judge from the ballad Sean O'Faolain prints in the *King of the Beggars,* O'Connell's message was well understood in the towns. Though vulgar and grotesque, the song reveals the impress of O'Connell: his fear of secret societies, hatred of sectarianism, as well as his conspicuous loyalty to the Throne.[203] Since they were the chief recipients of his propaganda, it is not surprising that the shopkeepers of Ireland understood him.

In the Gaelic mind, however, the Jacobite tradition persisted in the nineteenth century. This is to be seen in the Gaelic diary of the Callan schoolmaster, Humphrey O'Sullivan. Scientifically interested in nature, approving of the liberal revolts which periodically shatter the calm of Europe, articulate in his dislike of British rule in Ireland, O'Sullivan was typical of the new Irishman upon whom O'Connell depended.[204] Yet the past clung to the Callan schoolmaster. From the ideals of European liberalism his mind repeatedly slips back to the seventeenth century aspirations of the Gael.[205] In one of the fragmentary tales O'Sullivan left behind, the O'Neill, boasting descent from Niall of the Nine

[200] Sean O'Faolain, *op. cit.,* 294; Gwynn, *op. cit.,* 231-233.
[201] Doheny, *op. cit.,* 155; Denis Gwynn, *Young Ireland and 1848* (Cork, 1949), 226.
[202] Gwynn, *Young Ireland,* 253.
[203] O'Faolain, *op. cit.,* 221-223.
[204] *The Diary of Humphrey O'Sullivan;* Part I, IX-X.
[205] *Ibid.,* part I, 271. Also part II, 267, 275, 353; part III, 33.

Hostages, assures the hero that freedom is certain to come for "all the nations of the world, education is extending. The Rights of Man are being made clear . . . ."[206] However modern and cosmopolitan the forces making for liberation are, the O'Neill's real sympathies are more exclusive—"the children of the Gael" and the priests of God.[207] And his motives are anachronistic. He would strike off the Saxon shackles and make them pay for every "act of treachery and of wrongful theft of territory . . . ."[208]

The Aisling of Diarmuid O'Mahoney, popular Kerry poet, suggests that O'Connell was unable to wrench the Gaelic peasantry free from the Jacobite past. The poem prophecies that Repeal will come in 1845; not, however, by an act of Parliament, secured as a result of O'Connellite agitation; but according to the old dream of native pikes, aided by foreign invaders, with O'Connell himself leading the Gael against "Calvin's foreign flock."[209]

This is not to say that O'Connell's work was without significance for the peasantry. His was an immense figure and from it they selected that which had meaning for them. When the urbane and sympathetic author of the *Sportsman in Ireland* asked his guide what O'Connell had done for the people of Ireland, the peasant answered:

> We may have a light if we please now; and we walk about without being stopped by the soldiers; and it'll not be long before we get law and justice, and Catholic magistrates that will believe the truth from a Catholic. Oh! the devil fly away with Protestant magistrates that find all Catholics guilty.[210]

These were essentially the hopes O'Connell and his followers held before the Irish poor;[211] and in a great measure they were

---

[206] *Ibid.*, part IV, 141.
[207] *Ibid.*
[208] *Ibid.*, 143.
[209] Murphy, *op. cit.*, 20-21.
[210] *Sportsman in Ireland*, I, 173. The author was a partisan of O'Connell, defending him against the charges of the *Times* that he rack-rented his tenants.
[211] See speech of Humphrey O'Sullivan, defining Catholic Emancipation in a similar way. *Diary of Humphrey O'Sullivan*, part IV, 109 ff.

realized. No doubt there is bitter irony in O'Connell's parliamentary victories, but there were great gains too as a result in the administration of justice in county and borough. Perhaps because they could comprehend the realities of justice better than the abstractions of politics, the peasantry preferred the title "councillor" for O'Connell to that of Liberator.[212] They knew, in the words of the Callan schoolmaster, that "there is little use in going to law with the devil while the court is held in hell."[213] O'Connell, as John Mitchel said, "took all Ireland for his client,"[214] and if the peasants preferred to think of the great agitator as a shrewd and bombastic lawyer, their gains were none the less real for that.

If the peasantry of Ireland liked O'Connell for his earthy achievements those bookish young men whom he derisively called Young Irelanders did not. They disliked his appeals to the people's greed and the way in which he rested his arguments for Repeal upon the sordid logic of economics. "Passion and imagination have won victories which reason and self-interest would have attempted in vain," wrote Gavan Duffy, dignified chronicler of the movement which he helped found, "and it was on these subtle forces that the young men mainly counted."[215]

Though all of them would not have subscribed to John Mitchel's too vigorous indictment of O'Connell ("Poor old Dan! —wonderful, mighty, jovial and mean old man! with silver tongue and smile of witchery and heart of melting truth ....")[216] they did differ fundamentally from him in their conception of Ireland. To them the question of Repeal was not one of pressure politics, but the claim of a proud and historic nation to its own. "Though Englishmen were to give us the best tenures on earth," was the opinion of the brilliant Dublin *Nation,* newspaper organ of Young Ireland, "though they were to equalize Presbyterian, Catholic and Episcopalian, though they were to give us the completest representation in their Parliament . . . we would still tell

212 Duffy, *Young Ireland,* 40.
213 *Diary of Humphrey O'Sullivan,* part III, 5.
214 In O'Faolain, *op. cit.,* 118.
215 Duffy, *Young Ireland,* 65.
216 John Mitchel, *Jail Journal* (Dublin, 1918), 141.

them, in the name of enthusiastic hearts, thoughtful souls and fearless spirits that we spurned the offer if the condition were that Ireland were to remain a Province."[217]

Modern Irish nationalism begins to take shape with Young Ireland. On the political separation of Wolfe Tone they engrafted the notion of a distinctive Irish cultural tradition which enabled them to claim the status of a separate nationality. "Tone had set the feet of Ireland on a steep; Davis bade her in her journey remember her old honour and her old sanctity, the fame of Tara and Clonmacnois,"[218] Padraic Pearse wrote in 1916 a few months before he offered himself in sacrifice for the success of Ireland's journey. Thomas Davis and his followers did not mean simply to revive Gaelic-Catholic traditions, but to create an inclusive nationalism able and anxious to absorb all who "were to Ireland true" no matter their class, religion or origin.[219] Davis' fondness for the pseudonym "The Celt" does not reveal his race, for his was a family that considered itself English and he was Irish largely by choice, but rather his indebtedness to the mood of European Romanticism with its obsessive interest in the past.[220]

The Young Irelanders, however, were not mere antiquarians. They were interested in the past only insofar as it would serve the future. And Augustine Thierry in his *History of the Norman Conquest of England* had taught them how that might be done. The "father of modern history,"[221] as they called him, in his study entered the camp of the conquered rather than the Conqueror's and demonstrated how memories of the heroic past, cherished in song and legend sustained the courage of a conquered people and readied them for resurrection.[222] The responsibility of Young Ireland to unite all Irishmen did not permit them, how-

---

[217] Padraic H. Pearse, *The Spiritual Nation*. Tracts for the Times, No. 12 (Dublin, 1916)), 11; Charles Gavan Duffy, *Thomas Davis*, (London, 1890), 101.

[218] Pearse, *op. cit.*, 6.

[219] Tierney, "Thomas Davis," *op. cit.*, 306-307; Duffy, *Young Ireland*, 155-156.

[220] Tierney, *ibid.*, 301, 302, 307.

[221] Duffy, *Young Ireland*, 153.

[222] For Augustine Thierry see G. P. Gouch, *History and Historians in the Nineteenth Century* (New York, 1949), 170 ff. For Thierry's influence upon Young Ireland see article reprinted from *Temple Bar* in *Irish World*, February 5, 1881. Also *Irish Nation*, January 14, 1882; O'Leary, *op. cit.*, II, 83.

ever, to affirm a race war of the Celt against the Saxon or the Norman. The "Irish Thierry," Davis suggested, "must feel a love for all sects, a philosophical eye to the merits and demerits of all and haughty impartiality in speaking of all."[223]

Largely ignorant of Gaelic Ireland, and disdaining the common street ballads as unfit for the people, Young Ireland manufactured its own heroic literature. Davis, who had been trained for law, turned out scores of immensely popular ballads and songs which were to serve nationalists in Ireland and America for generations to come. The poet Yeats would later have to fight one of his first literary battles against the Young Ireland tradition of literature as propaganda.[224]

Young Ireland also looked to formal histories and biographies for sparks to ignite the fires of Irish patriotism. For history, properly read, bore the stamp of the national character and was able to fill the national mind with noble thoughts. And these, Davis said in an impassioned address to the Historical Society in 1840 from which we may date the beginning of Young Ireland, "are more enriching than mines of gold . . . more supporting in dangers hour than colonies or fleets . . . ."[225] Irish history had long been ignored as nothing but a dreary chronicle of cattle raids and broken heads, but the young romantics, undaunted and with marvelous energy, set out to recreate the Irish past. John O'Donovan, the fine Irish scholar and antiquarian, in a letter to Davis complained of historical distortions. "It may be useful just now to talk of long faded glories," he wrote, "but it is my opinion that we have but few national glories to boast of in our history . . . ."[226] The nationalists, however, were less concerned with historical accuracy than with their ability to persuade the Irish people that only when they separated themselves from "the men, feelings and interests of England"[227] will they be on the road to freedom.

It is ironic therefore that Young Ireland's ideals should be

---

[223] Rolleston, *op. cit.*, 90, 222.
[224] William Butler Yeats, *The Autobiography of William Butler Yeats*, (New York, 1938), 176-177.
[225] Duffy, *Davis*, 33.
[226] In Duffy, *Davis*, 209-210.
[227] Griffith, *Davis*, 12.

derived largely from the English Romantics, from Scott and from Wordsworth and Landor;[228] that Young Ireland's ideas should be common to or inspired by conservative English critics of Utilitarianism. For Thomas Davis the ethical system of Bishop Butler, Anglican defender of revealed religion in the eighteenth century, was more inspiring than the utilitarian ethics of Paley, just as it was for the anti-Benthamites at Cambridge and Oxford.[229]

Hatred for what Davis called the "filthy dungeon" of Utilitarianism was as common to Young England as it was to Young Ireland.[230] Both groups of nationalists sought the cement for a new nationalism in the traditions of the past;[1] and both shared a common prophet in Thomas Carlyle.[231] Perhaps it was in recognition of these mutual attitudes that Young Englanders, during the years when they served under the colorful if unstable banner of Disraeli, offered Ireland their sympathies and often their Parliamentary votes.[232]

Carlyle was the special hero of Young Ireland. "Our Thomas," they called him; and though he said harsh things about Ireland, the serious young men loved him because he valued the compulsions of Duty above the selfish hedonism of the "Pig Philosophy."[233] Carlyle's influence was particularly marked upon John Mitchel. The furious prose of his *Jail Journal* reveals the debt he owed to the dour Scotchman and perhaps also to Cobbett; and Mitchel's wild defiance of the government in 1847 and 1848 may have been due, as Gavan Duffy says, to a too literal acceptance of Carlyle's theory of the spontaneity of a people's revolt against oppression.[234] Certainly, Mitchel's heroic rejection of in-

---

[228] Duffy, *Davis,* 40 says that Landor and Wordsworth were for Davis "familar companions of his solitude."

[229] Duffy, *Davis,* 19; Ernest Campbell Mossner, *Bishop Butler and the Age of Reason* (New York, 1936), 198-211.

[230] Duffy, *Davis,* 76, 83; Griffith, *Davis,* V-VIII; William Flavelle Monypenny, *The Life of Benjamin Disraeli, Earl of Beaconsfield* (New York, 1917), II, 162-172.

[231] Emery Neff, *Carlyle and Mill* (New, York, 1926), 309-310.

[232] Duffy, *Four Years of Irish History,* 372, 451; Duffy, *Young Ireland,* 451-452; Monypenny, *op. cit.,* 171-173.

[233] Duffy, *Four Years of Irish History,* 84; Duffy, *Young Ireland,* 736-737; William Dillon, *Life of John Mitchel* (London, 1888), I, 105.

[234] Duffy, *Four Years of Irish History,* 552.

dustrial civilization, in America as in Great Britain, followed the pattern of Carlyle's thought.[235]

For Young Ireland, nationalism and anti-Utilitarianism were identical. Utilitarianism is believed and preached everywhere, wrote Thomas Davis to a friend in 1842, "and threatens to crorupt the lower classes who are still *faithful* and *romantic*. To use every literary and political engine against this seems to me to be the first duty of an Irish patriot." Rather than submit, Davis would "hazard open war" and "if we failed it would be in our own power before dying to throw up huge barriers against English vices, and dying, to leave example and a religion to the next age."[236] Significantly, it was the tragic inability of the government, blinded as it was by Benthamite economics, to halt the Great Famine that led Young Ireland to rise in revolt.

"I shall stand by Old Ireland," O'Connell once roared in an unhappy debate with Davis, "and I have some slight notion that Old Ireland will stand by me."[237] He was right, of course. Part of Young Ireland's appeal lay in the newness of their doctrines,[238] but the peasant was a traditionalist and suspicious of the new. When the young nationalists broke with O'Connell in 1846, they lost contact with the rural masses;[239] as a result the Rising of 1848 was a comic failure.

Aware of the peasant's traditional hatred for England, and believing him faithful to the romantic past, Young Ireland hoped that the shimmering ideal of national freedom would inspire the people to join them in revolt. Michael Doheny, as he left home to join his fellow rebels, felt no doubts: "From earliest childhood to that hour, I never met one Irishman whose hope it was not to deliver the country forever from English thrall."[240] The fiery mass meetings of the previous weeks and the often wild enthusi-

---

[235] For Mitchel's criticism of American worship of the dollar and his support of slavery see Dillon, *ibid.*, 281-282, 337-338; II, 46-49, 56, 60-61.

[236] Letter to D. O. Maddyn, July 24, 1842 in Duffy, *Davis*, 83.

[237] In Duffy, *Young Ireland*, 705.

[238] R.C.K. Ensor, "Some Political and Economic Interactions in Later Victorian England," in R. L. Schuyler and Herman Ausubel, edd. *The Making of English History* (New York, 1952), 539.

[239] Duffy, *Four Years of Irish History*, 263, 245, 591, 595.

[240] Doheny, *The Felon's Track*, 160.

asm of the people upon the appearance of the insurgents must have increased his confidence.

The handsome and terribly romantic Thomas F. Meagher has left a description—one worthy of Carlyle—of the way he was received when he rode into the town of Carrick, pistol and sword proclaiming his purpose and green ribbon his cause. "A torrent of human beings," he wrote, ". . . whirling in dizzy circles . . . with sounds of wrath, vengeance and defiance . . . invocations, sobs and thrilling wailings . . . scornful, exulting delirious defiances of death; all wild as the winter gusts at sea."[241]

The people, however, did not fight. Bewildered perhaps because their songs threatened to come to life, they listened and cheered, but never obeyed. The Rising ended with token bloodletting in a cabbage garden at Ballingarry, where the rebels proved themselves gentlemen if not serious revolutionaries. And Doheny, after following the "Felon's Track" to safety away from Ireland, bitterly blessed the "wildest waves that bear me from a land of slaves."[242] Young Ireland had fallen into the chasm that lay between peasant thought and peasant rhetoric.

Poverty and hunger, as Meagher thought, undoubtedly sapped the courage of the people.[243] Yet hunger was not new to Ireland, and its shadow had invariably given desperate courage to the peasant secret societies. James Fintan Lalor, queer, hunch-backed revolutionary, with a plan too bold for his times, had warned Young Ireland that the Irish peasant was a "wolf-dog," but that for "Repeal indeed he will never bite but only bay . . . ."[244] For possession of a piece of land, Lalor insisted, the peasants would bite and bite savagely; and he urged a social revolution that would claim the land for the people.[245]

For the majority of Young Irelanders, conservative in thought, fearful of a Jacquerie, and anxious to convert the landlords to nationalism, Lalor's scheme was poor strategy and worse

---

[241] Meagher's narrative of the Rising in Gwynn, *Young Ireland and 1848*, Appendix 1, 296.

[242] Doheny, *Felon's Track*, 271. For similar reactions from the other rebels, see the narratives in Gwynn, *ibid.*

[243] Gwynn, *ibid.*, 286-287.

[244] Duffy, *Four Years of Irish History*, 469.

[245] *Ibid.*, 498-499.

ethics.[246] During the Rising, Smith O'Brien was ludicrously faithful to the rights of private property, refusing to permit the people to seize provisions, or even to fell trees for a barricade without permission of the owners. In this way the gulf between their hopes and his became apparent and the peasant mobs melted away.[247] For the peasant in Limerick in 1848, as in Mayo fifty years earlier, the game was not worth the candle. As one anonymous rebel put it, "The horizon of their thoughts was bounded by the parish in which they lived, or at best by the county and an Irish nation was a phrase to which no real meaning was attached."[248]

But the influence of Young Ireland did not die in 1848. Old Ireland commanded that year, but the future belonged to the heirs of Thomas Davis. As he had hoped, he left "example and a religion to the next age." His ideas and songs crossed to the New World with the Famine ships. And there the burden of Irish nationalism was to be borne for the next half-century; for in the alembic of America the parochial peasant was transformed into a passionate Irish nationalist.

------

[246] *Ibid.*, 470 ff.
[247] Gwynn, *Young Ireland and 1848*, 317.
[248] Duffy, *ibid.*, 690.

IRISH NATIONALISM AND IRISH CATHOLICISM

A Study in Cultural Identity

Lawrence J. McCaffrey

Irish Nationalism and Irish Catholicism:
A Study In Cultural Identity

LAWRENCE J. MCCAFFREY

What matters that at different shrines
We pray unto one God?
What matters that at different times
Our fathers won this sod?
In fortune and in name we're bound
By stronger links than steel;
And neither can be safe nor sound
But in the other's weal.

—Thomas Davis

Seven years ago the Irish people celebrated the fiftieth anniversary of the Easter Monday Rebellion: the "Blood Sacrifice" that inspired the Anglo-Irish War leading to the Treaty, the Free State and finally the Republic. During the festivities, politicians paid homage to the memory of Padraig Pearse, James Connolly and their colleagues in the Volunteer and Citizen Armies; towns and villages erected monuments to men who died for Irish freedom; professional and amateur historians produced volumes of description and analyses of the brave deeds of Easter Week; bands played and singers sang patriotic airs; and someone blew up Nelson's Pillar in O'Connell Street. A prominent politician, a hero of 1916, allegedly described the last event in newspaper headline style as "noted British admiral leaves Dublin by air." The 1916 commemoration was more than a hymn to the past; it was also a tribute to the values and successes of physical force nationalism. Ireland in 1966 seemed a model of productive revolution: a stable community with viable democratic institutions and an expanding economy; an example for other countries emancipated from the scourge of imperialism. This was the consensus of a confident nation.

In 1973 there is a more reflective mood in Ireland. A number of intelligent people question the dividends of revolution and violence. Back in 1966, *Studies,* a scholarly Jesuit quarterly, decided not to publish an essay by the Reverend Francis Shaw, because his thesis contradicted the spirit of celebration. Father Shaw has since died, but his view of Irish history now seems relevant to the editors of *Studies,* and his essay has been published in a recent issue of the journal. Shaw attacked the revolutionary theories of Wolfe Tone and Pearse and their impact on Irish thought and action. He condemned the "myth" that the men of 1916 redeemed their people from the failures, decadence and West Britonism of constitutional nationalism.[1] Another sign of revisionism in community values was

This paper was read before a joint session of the American Historical Association and the American Committee for Irish Studies at New Orleans, December 30, 1972.

1. Francis Shaw, S.J., ''The Canon of Irish History—A Challenge,'' *Studies* 61 (Summer 1972):113-153. Shaw's case reflects a clerical perspective. He condemned Tone as a man who admired French Revolutionary ideology and hated England more than he loved Ireland or her peasant masses. He also emphasized Tone's antagonism to things Catholic. Shaw deplored Pearse's confusion of Celtic pagan mythology with Christian doctrine and holiness with patriotism. This muddled thinking involved Christianity as an accessory in two moral evils: blood letting and hatred between peoples. Shaw insisted that

Mr. McCaffrey is professor of history in Loyola University of Chicago, Illinois.

1

the contents of the papers and lectures presented to the August 1972 Merriman Summer School in Scariff, County Clare. Distinguished scholars praised Daniel O'Connell's contributions to the rise of Irish nationalism and the development of liberal democratic values in the consciences of the Irish people. Perhaps the day is not too far distant when John Redmond's reputation will enjoy a similar restoration.

This reappraisal of constitutional versus revolutionary nationalism is the product of current troubles in Northern Ireland. Turbulence and violence in the Six Counties has compacted centuries of Irish history into a few short years: Protestant bigotry, Catholic desperation, the irresponsibility and insensitivity of British politicians, British soldiers shooting Irishmen, Irish revolutionaries sniping at and ambushing British soldiers, curfews, coercion and internment. Reasonable nationalists are almost as appalled by Irish Republican Army Provisionals exploding bombs that maim and kill innocent bystanders as they are by Tommies gunning down Catholic civilians or Protestant murder gangs using assassination as a terror weapon. Friends of the IRA insist that violence has forced a British concern with and concessions to minority grievances. They refuse to acknowledge the fact that it has also strengthened the political and psychological walls of Partition by intensifying sectarian bitterness. The logic of 1916 no longer seems infallible. Events in the North have also focused attention on another controversial subject in Irish history: the complicated relationship between Irish nationalism and Irish Catholicism.

Concentrating on the adjectives, American and British newspapers tend to describe the conflict in Northern Ireland as a religious war, a throwback to the savagery of the seventeenth century. Statements from Protestant Unionist leaders seem to verify this interpretation. They say that the alternative solutions to the crisis in their part of Ulster are Protestant freedom within the United Kingdom or Catholic despotism within a United Ireland. They use old slogans like "Home Rule is Rome Rule." Whether they are members of the Official or Provisional IRA, the Democratic Social Labour Party, or the Northern Ireland Civil Rights Association, Catholics avoid sectarian rhetoric in explaining their aims. They reject Protestant charges that the objectives of both the civil rights and nationalist efforts are directed at Catholic ascendancy in a United Ireland. Even William Cardinal Conway, archbishop of Armagh and Catholic primate, a most conservative prelate, refers to the issues in Northern Ireland as "basically political, social, and economic" in nature.[2] Cardinal Conway, revolutionary and constitutional nationalists and civil righters are not manufacturing propaganda to beguile British and world opinion. Their rejection of sectarian ambitions is consistent with the liberal democratic traditions of Irish nationalism.

Enlisting the priest as an agent of agitation, Daniel O'Connell constructed modern Irish nationalism out of the bricks of Catholic discontent, but he borrowed the rhetoric of his movement from the Whig, natural rights principles of John Locke. He admired the eighteenth-century Anglo-Irish Protestant patriots and the American founding fathers who utilized those principles to expand the free-

abstract ideological nationalism was never a feature of the Irish mentality: "The Irishman fought for his religious beliefs, he fought for his home and land, and he fought for life itself or the food to sustain that life, but he did not belong to the world in which national sovereignty was maintained by standing armies; the Irish national consciousness was more subtle, more spiritual and, I am glad to say, more peaceful" (p. 145).
2. *Newsweek* (European Edition), September 4, 1972, p. 56.

dom of their countries. But O'Connell traveled beyond the frontiers of Whig patriotism. He was one of the leading Benthamites in the United Kingdom Parliament of the 1830s and 1840s. Working from Radical premises, O'Connell pledged that an independent Ireland would be a democratic society with full civil liberties and freedom of conscience for all citizens. Defending separation of church and state as essential for individual liberty, he rejected Catholic power as a substitute for Protestant ascendancy. He constantly courted Protestant cooperation in his campaigns to create a prosperous and harmonious Irish nation: "The Protestant alone could not expect to liberate his country—the Roman Catholic alone could not do it—neither could the Presbyterian—but amalgamate the three into the Irishman, and the Union is repealed."[3]

All significant Irish freedom movements after O'Connell retained the liberal commitment he injected into the spirit of nationalism. Young Irelanders pleaded for the union of Anglo-Irish and Celt, Protestant and Catholic in a common struggle against Anglo-Saxon political and cultural tyranny. Charles Gavan Duffy, Frederick Lucas, Sir Edward Grey and George Henry Moore launched the independent Irish party of the 1850s to agitate tenant right as a way of bringing Catholic and Protestant peasants together in mutual interest, a precursor of a non-denominational nationalist movement. The contents of the Fenian proclamation of an Irish Republic, published in *The Times* (London) on March 8, 1867, clearly showed that a liberal democratic, non-sectarian Ireland was as much an objective of physical force as it was of constitutional nationalism:

We aim at founding a republic based on universal suffrage, which shall secure to all the intrinsic value of their labour. The soil of Ireland at present in the possession of an oligarchy belongs to us, the Irish people, and to us it must be restored. We declare also in favour of absolute liberty of conscience, and the separation of Church and State.

In 1870 Isaac Butt initiated the Home Rule movement to enlist Protestant resentment against Gladstone's Irish reforms, disestablishment and the land act. In his long pamphlet, *Irish Federalism* (1870), he promised his coreligionists that their property and political influence would best be protected by an Irish Parliament in which they would be the dominant element. According to Butt, Irish Catholics were of a conservative disposition, eager to follow the lead of the Protestant aristocracy in an effort to restore the Irish nation. He preached an Irish Christian crusade—Catholic and Protestant—against the dangerous threats of British radicalism and secularism. Butt projected two kinds of Ireland: one a self-governing island fortress of Christian and conservative values in a pagan, radical sea; the other bearing the burdens and sharing the glories of the mighty British empire.

Charles Stewart Parnell, Butt's successor as Home Rule leader, also spoke of the common bonds uniting Irish Catholic and Protestant. He said that the national movement needed the "patriotism, and the talent and the work of every Irishman", and that the Protestant minority would be a significant and "moderating influence" in the Irish nation.[4] John Redmond and John Dillon, the last two leaders of the Irish parliamentary party, so scrupulously maintained the liberal and ecumenical doctrines of Irish nationalism that a few members of the Irish and

3. Speech before aggregate meeting, September 18, 1810, *The Select Speeches of Daniel O'Connell*, ed. John O'Connell (Dublin, 1846), 1:23.
4. Robert Kee, *The Green Flag* (London, 1972), p. 403.

British Catholic hierarchies complained that Home Rule was an inadequate expression of Catholic aspirations.

Easter Week rebels also insisted on a nationalism free from sectarianism. Their *Proclamation* to the Irish people said that,

The Irish Republic is entitled to and hereby claims the allegiance of every Irishman and Irishwoman. The Republic guarantees religious and civil liberty, equal rights and equal opportunities to all its citizens, and declares its resolve to pursue the happiness and prosperity of the whole nation and of all its parts, cherishing all the children of the nation equally, and oblivious of the differences carefully fostered by an alien government, which have divided a minority from the majority in the past.

Post-Treaty Irish nationalist politicians wrote constitutions fulfilling the pledges of their predecessors. In the Irish Republic there is a separation of church and state with full civil rights for all citizens. Protestants play an important role in the cultural, social and economic life of the community. Their share of the national wealth far exceeds their population statistics. Some of them have been and still are important politicians. To the credit of Irish nationalism, the position of Protestants in the Republic contrasts favorably with the beleagured status of Catholics in Northern Ireland.

Despite the liberal ecumenical convictions of its theoreticians, Irish nationalism never became inclusive. Thomas Davis was wrong: it did matter at what "different shrines we pray unto one God" and when "our fathers won this sod." These things counted because religion in Ireland was and is much more than theology and liturgy; it involves identity. The Reformation erected a permanent barrier between British and Irish. Religion was an important ingredient in the sixteenth- and seventeenth-centuries survival conflict between the Gaelic and invading English cultures. Catholicism became a symbol of a besieged way of life; Protestantism was an alien force, part of the process of conquest and imperialism. The English won the war, and their garrison, Anglo-Irish Protestants, deprived Catholics of civil, religious and property rights, reducing most of them to the level of serfs. Ireland was two communities: Protestant and Catholic, conqueror and conquered, master and serf. With a few exceptions it is correct to say that religion served as the demarcation line separating those with power from the powerless, those with property from the dispossed.

Most cultural nationalists quickly reject the suggestion that Catholicism is the main ingredient in the Irish personality. Daniel Corkery, perhaps the most influential philosopher of twentieth-century Irish cultural nationalism, insisted that the uniqueness of Gaelic culture was even more important than Catholic loyalties in creating an identity that carried the Irish through the dark days of bondage. In *The Hidden Ireland* (1925), Corkery described eighteenth-century Irish speaking peasants living under thatch roofs of dirt-floored, windowless, smoky cottages and reciting poems reflecting the values of a once rich medieval Celtic civilization. According to Corkery, this heritage gave the people an inner pride and fortitude, masked by the survival obsequiousness of serfdom.

In the "Proem" of his O'Connell biography, *King of the Beggars* (1938), Sean O'Faolain, once a Corkery disciple, confronted his old master's thesis that Gaelic culture survived as a dynamic identity and messianic influence in the lives of the peasantry. O'Faolain argued that ancient Gaelic culture represented the values of an extinct aristocratic clan society. Eighteenth-century poets, the descendents of bards, were wandering tramps, shebeen owners, hedge school masters or tillers of fields, but they sang of the halls of Gaelic kings or exiled Stuarts returning as liberators. The two songs, one a memory, the other a fantasy, had little to say to demoralized, almost dehumanized, impoverished serfs. Their only meaningful symbol of identity, their only real possession, was a religious faith that brought some beauty to ugly lives, some hope in a desperate situation. As O'Faolain put it, the Catholicism of the Irish peasant was "not an inconsiderable possession. . . . They had, in a word, with that one exception of their faith, nothing, neither a present, nor a past, nor a future."[5] Catholicism was their main nourishment as they started on a long march toward freedom and dignity.

Catholic liturgy was the mortar cementing the Irish community, touching all the essential aspects of life—birth, marriage, sickness, death: the moments that provide purpose and meaning in the existence of both humble and famous people. In the words of Patrick O'Farrell, Irish Catholicism was more "than the official pronouncements of the hierarchy: it is a set of values, a culture, a historical tradition, a view on the world, a disposition of mind and heart, a loyalty, an emotion, a psychology—and a nationalism."[6] O'Farrell's observations are equally valid for the mentality and personality of the Irish Protestant community.

Irish attitudes did not necessarily have to be frozen in a Reformation, Counter Reformation context. Irish nationalism could have become inclusive rather than exclusive. Catholic leaders did renounce revenge intentions. They sought the friendship and cooperation of Protestants. Unfortunately their overtures met rejection. Anglo-Irish Protestants contributed patriotic rhetoric and the memory of a nation to the contents of Irish nationalism. But as Robert Kee, *The Green Flag* (1972), has shown, the Protestant concept of the Irish nation excluded Catholics who were to remain in a servile condition. Despite the myths of Irish nationalism, Anglo-Irish patriotism was more Protestant than Irish. In *The Irish* Sean O'Faolain describes the Anglo-Irish community as a separate enclave: "They resided in Ireland—their country never their nation—so that their achievements were, for the most part, so remote from the life of the native Irish (now utterly suppressed) that they ultimately became part of the English rather than the Irish cultural record."[7]

Irish nationalist mythology represents Theobold Wolfe Tone as an example of unselfish Protestant nationalism. Tone was the most prominent and talented member of the Protestant middle class Society of United Irishmen, founded in 1791. Inspired by the rationalism, optimism and secularism of the Enlightenment, United Irishmen tried to forge an alliance between Protestant middle class Radicals, Catholic gentry and middle classes seeking civil rights and Catholic peasants (the Defenders) demanding an end to manorialism. United Irishmen started as political reformers demanding an Irish Parliament subject to the influence of a democratic public opinion. Frustrated by government oppression and encouraged by Jacobin success in France, Tone and his friends moved from reform to revolution. When

5. Sean O'Faolain, *King of the Beggars* (London, 1938), p. 29.
6. Patrick O'Farrell, *Ireland's English Question* (New York, 1972), p. 306. O'Farrell's book is based on a thesis that religion is the fundamental issue dividing Britain from Ireland. He insists that Catholicism shaped the Irish personality and is the essence of Irish nationalism. He argues that the liberal democratic values of Repeal and Home Rule nationalism were alien in character and irrelevant in the Irish situation. O'Farrell's insights are often brilliant but he tends to be more the advocate than the historian and distorts the realities of both Catholicism and nationalism.
7. Sean O'Faolain, *The Irish* (London, 1969), p. 88.

it came in 1798, Irish revolution exposed sectarian hatred rather than mutual effort. Catholics in Wexford attempted, with some success, to exterminate Protestant landlords. Their coreligionists in Mayo joined Humbert's French invaders to fight for the pope and the Blessed Virgin. Protestant United Irishmen in Ulster more often expressed the bigotry of the Orange lodges than the tolerance of Wolfe Tone.

In the late 1790s a significant number of Protestants abandoned patriotism to endorse a Union with Britain. They wanted a shield to protect Protestant ascendancy from the threat of an alliance between Catholic discontent, United Irishmen Protestant middle class radicalism and the military power of France. Many of the Protestants opposing the Union were as selfishly motivated as those promoting the British connection. They were convinced that a Protestant Irish Parliament would be more vigilant in suppressing Catholic protest than a remote, perhaps more objective, United Kingdom legislature.

During the 1820s, 1830s and 1840s O'Connell's successes in organizing and sustaining mass agitations for Catholic Emancipation and Repeal of the Union revived Irish Protestant paranoia. The Home Rule movement and its alliance with British Liberalism in the 1880s completed the Protestant retreat into the garrison mentality of the early eighteenth century. Although there were Protestants like Henry Grattan, Thomas Davis, William Smith O'Brien, Isaac Butt and Charles Stewart Parnell who believed Ireland more important than class or sect, the Protestant community was increasingly committed to the Union as protection against the victory of a Catholic democracy threatening its control over property and political influence. Protestants equated their religious faith to their Unionist allegiance. It was the flag of their cultural identity: British not Irish.

British no-Popery contributed as much, perhaps more, to the Catholic, Irish twin identities than the persecution mania of Anglo-Irish Protestants. The progress of Irish nationalism made the Irish question the most emotional issue in British politics: the Union became the rallying point for aristocratic privileges, property rights, the Empire and the "Protestant Constitution." British politicians, mostly Conservatives, exploited the antipathy of British public opinion toward things Catholic as a weapon to gain or maintain office and preserve the status quo.[8] They insisted that Irish nationalism and Irish Catholicism were inseparable forces aiming at the integrity of the United Kingdom and the Empire. Conservatives, in a desperate effort to defeat Liberal reform through its alliance with Irish nationalism, inflamed the irrational prejudices of British and Irish Protestants, particularly in northeast Ulster. They played the "Orange Card"—"Ulster will fight and Ulster will be right"—even to the precipice of civil war.

Hatreds encouraged years ago by British politicians like Randolph Churchill, F. E. Smith and Andrew Bonar Law still inflame the passions of the Protestant majority in Northern Ireland. Protestants of all classes claim they are making a last gallant stand for British culture against papist tyranny, ignorance and subversion, all represented by Irish nationalism. Protestant nationalism in the Six

8. British no-Popery, anti-Irish nativism is analyzed and discussed in Gilbert Cahill's "Irish Catholicism and English Toryism," *Review of Politics* 19 (January 1957):62-76, and "The Protestant Association and the Anti-Maynooth Agitation of 1845," *Catholic Historical Review* 43 (October 1957):273-308. During the preparation of this essay, I had the good fortune of reading Professor Cahill's book length manuscript, "Popery, Nativism, and Nationalism in Great Britain: The British Reaction to the Irish Question, 1800-1848." E. R. Norman, *Anti-Catholicism in Victorian England* (New York, 1968), also discusses nineteenth-century British xenophobia in relationship to Catholicism.

Counties is more racial and cultural than sectarian. In addition to the insults
—"Pope heads", "Teagues", "bloody Micks", "Fenians"—Protestants tell their
children that Catholics are inherently filthy, treacherous, violent and improvident.
They say that Catholics "are trained to use every device to get money without
working. Their priests tell them to have large families so that they will out-
number us at the polls and swamp the welfare rolls. So they breed like rabbits."[9]
Many members of the Protestant counterpart to the IRA, the Ulster Defense
Association, believe that Catholics must be driven out of Northern Ireland: "You
can't trust them. There can be no peace until there is one community."[10] This
Ulster Protestant contempt for Catholics reflects fear more than arrogance—the
old garrison insecurity. After almost four centuries they still feel like strangers
in the land. They are convinced that the natives, the real Irish, the Catholic Irish,
are bent on vengence. And they have no confidence in the sticking power of the
British in a touchy situation. Protestant anxiety has been translated into fifty
years of brutal oppression which has now been answered by violent resistance.[11]

Emigration was another factor securing the bonds between Irish and Catholic,
Anglo-Saxon and Protestant. Irishmen of the diaspora, refugees in Britain and
pioneers of the American ghettoes contributed money and intensity to the cause
of Irish freedom. Much of the nationalist fervor that flowed into Anglo-Irish
relations from across the Irish Sea and Atlantic Ocean was a response to religious
discrimination. The immigrants' Catholicism, their offensive poverty culture and
their skill in acquiring political influence irritated the no-Popery sensibilities of
Anglo-Saxon Protestant nativism. Americans and Britons treated the Irish as
pariahs endangering the purity, survival and dominance of Anglo-Saxon institutions and values.[12] To achieve and maintain dignity in hostile environments, Irish
refugees and their descendents cultivated political and cultural nationalism. They
aided liberation movements back home and looked forward to the day when an independent Ireland would elevate their status in Britain and the United States.[13]

9. Interview with Jim McDonald, member of the Orange Order in Belfast, by Gary Mac-
Eoin, *Chicago Today*, October 23, 1972. McDonald believes that Catholic strategy in
Northern Ireland is planned in the Vatican because the pope fears that Communists
will take over Italy and he wants to use a United Catholic Ireland as a base to launch
an offensive to give the church world domination.
10. *Ibid.*
11. Recently there have been a number of interesting studies on the crisis in Northern Ireland, but it is difficult for historians, sociologists and political scientists to probe and
expose the attitudes of Six County Protestants and Catholics. Creative writers often do
a better job of character analysis and revelation. Joseph Tomelty, *The Apprentice* (1953),
Brian Moore, *The Lonely Passion of Judith Hearne* (1955), *The Feast of Lupercal*
1958) and *The Emperor of Ice Cream* (1965) and the poetry of Seumas Heaney and
John Montague describe the Catholic mentality and persecution complex. In an age
when civil rights are an international concern, the Catholic minority is a more sympathetic
group than the Orange faction, and most of the writing talent resides in the Catholic
community. The Protestant ascendancy is ''An ugly race. . . . No poet will ever sing for
them—of them'' (Maurice Leitch, *Poor Lazarus* (1969), p. 186). But two Protestant
writers, Maurice Leitch, *Poor Lazarus* and *Liberty Lad* (1965), and Robert Harbinson,
No Surrender (1960), *Song of Erne* (1960) and *Up Spake the Cabin Boy* (1961) have
revealed the fears, anxieties, violence and alienation of the Ulster Protestant community.
12. British and American Anglo-Saxon, Protestant anti-Catholicism evolving into racism
has been defined and described by Ray Allen Billington, *The Protestant Crusade, 1800-
1860* (New York, 1938), John Higham, *Strangers in the Land: Patterns of American
Nativism, 1860-1925* (New York, 1965), John Archer Jackson, *The Irish in Britain*
(London, 1963) and L. P. Curtis, Jr., *Anglo-Saxons and Celts: A Study in Anti-Irish
Prejudice in Victorian England* (Bridgeport, 1968).
13. Irish-American nationalism as reaction to American nativism has been discussed by
Thomas N. Brown, ''The Origins and Character of Irish-American Nationalism,'' *Review
of Politics* 18 (July 1956):327-358, and *Irish-American Nationalism* (New York, 1967);
and Lawrence J. McCaffery, ''Pioneers of the American Ghetto,'' *Illinois Quarterly* 34
(September 1971):31-42.

As the pressures from nativist hate and their own psychological insecurity forced immigrants to huddle together in ghetto shelters, they had to accept the definition of their enemies: they were Irish, they were Catholic, and the two were one.

The intimate relationship between Irish and Catholic has imposed burdens and limitations on both identities. Irish Catholicism has frequently prevented Irish nationalism from achieving the cosmopolitanism defined by its founders and claimed by its spokesmen. The Catholic church does have an unhealthy influence in the affairs of the Republic. Article 44 of the 1937 constitution recognized "the special position of the Holy Catholic Apostolic and Roman Church as the guardian of the Faith possessed by the great majority of the citizens."[14] The constitution also makes Catholic teachings on marriage and the family the law of the land. Acting on this premise, the Dail has banned the sale of contraceptives.

Critics of life in the Republic claim that liberal democratic institutions camouflage clericalism. Defending Partition, Prime Minister Heath of Great Britain has described the Republic as a theocracy.[15] Many people with Irish nationalist and liberal Catholic credentials have expressed similar sentiments. Sean O'Casey, Protestant, Socialist and nationalist, referred to the Roman Catholic seminary at Maynooth as "the brain, the body, the nerve and the tissue of the land, controlling two thirds of the country, influencing it all."[16] Protesting the role of the hierarchy in preventing enactment of a vital health measure in 1951, Sean O'Faolain complained that there were two parliaments in Ireland, one operating out of Maynooth, the other from Dublin. The former was not subject to the pressures of public opinion and held the ultimate weapon in its bid for supremacy over the lay legislature: the faith of the Catholic masses in the church's essential role in the salvation process.[17] Recently, Dr. Noel Browne, former Minister for Health in the 1948-1951 coalition government and a victim of the hierarchy's intrusion into the parliamentary arena, has insisted that Protestants in the North do have reason to be apprehensive concerning the possibility of a United Ireland. According to Browne, the Catholic church in the Republic enjoys a virtual monopoly in the field of education and an undemocratic, conservative influence over social thought, services and legislation.[18] At the present time letters and editorials published in Irish newspapers demand that the Dail secularize the constitution and repeal laws that might antagonize the private consciences of non-Catholics. Members of the Catholic hierarchy seem to accept the deletion of article 44 from the constitution, but they probably would fight hard to retain the ban on divorce and restrictions against birth control. Recently, Dr. Daly, bishop of Ardagh and Clonmacnoise, insisted that the state must maintain the permanence of marriage and prevent contraception, not as questions of religion, but as an obligation to sustain the social fabric of the community.[19]

Clerical power is an obvious fact of Irish life, but John Whyte, *Church and State in Modern Ireland* (1971), has presented ample evidence to show that Ire-

14. Recently the Irish people by plebiscite overwhelmingly voted to eliminate article 44 from the constitution. The voter turnout, however, was light.
15. *New York Times*, February 27, 1972.
16. Sean O'Casey, *Innisfallen Fare Thee Well* (New York, 1949), pp. 320-321.
17. Sean O'Faolain, "The Dail and the Bishop," *The Bell* (June 1951):5-13.
18. *Irish Times*, August 19, 1972.
19. *Ibid.*, August 12, 1972. Cardinal Conway in his September 4, 1972 *Newsweek* interview assured Protestants that in a United Ireland they would be permitted to follow their consciences on such matters as divorce and birth control. The implication of the Cardinal's statement is that Catholics would not have such an opportunity. He does not explain how the state could make such distinctions in law.

land is far from a theocracy. Clericalism is effective only when it harmonizes with the climate of national opinion. Most Irish citizens are committed to the liberal democratic traditions of Irish nationalism. They do not tolerate Catholic frustrations of national objectives or clerical interference in areas clearly political. But that is the problem! What is clearly political? Where do economics, political science and sociology start, and religious values and ethical codes leave off? Many societies find it difficult to distinguish between the things of God and those of Caesar. In Ireland the dilemma is particularly acute. Ninety-five percent of the population is Catholic, and most Irish Catholics are devout in the practice of their religion. The church and her ministers have always been an essential part of Irish life. In the bad days priests were close to the people, sharing their poverty and degradation. They were the leading targets for British and Anglo-Irish no-Popery, anti-Irish prejudice. They were the only educated leaders in rural peasant communities. Laymen accepted them as advisors and authorities on a wide range of topics. Because of their influence, nationalist politicians recruited the priests as agitators and organizers. There never was a distinction in the varied roles of a clergyman: minister of the Gospel, protector of his flock, local agent of nationalism. Priests preached Repeal, tenant right and Home Rule as well as Catholic doctrine and morality from the pulpit. They were not likely to surrender their diverse authority in national life with the coming of an Irish Parliament; and laymen were hesitant to withdraw their deference from a class of men who long symbolized Ireland's resistance to Anglo-Saxon conquest and control and represented the important religious aspect of Irish culture.

Irish nationalism must also bear considerable responsibility for blurring the lines that should separate the cities of God and man. In order not to alienate potential recruits, nationalists constantly refused to add social and economic dimensions to their ideology. They argued that the quest for social justice within the context of nationalism would divide Ireland on class and religious lines at the expense of consensus and unity.[20] A free Ireland was the panacea for all grievances; an Irish Parliament would reconcile all differences. In this futile bid for Protestant support, Irish nationalism left a vacuum of ideas that was filled by the church. Bishops and priests, supported by pious laymen, insisted that the social and economic instructions contained in papal encyclicals and the essays of Thomist philosophers and moral theologians must be the proper guidelines for a Christian community. They claimed "that the Church is the Divinely appointed guardian and interpreter of the moral law" and that they were the consciences of the nation.[21]

20. Fenianism is perhaps the best example of the reluctance of Irish nationalism to become involved with social reform. James Stephens and John O'Mahoney, the cofounders of the Irish Republican Brotherhood, became sympathetic to socialism during their post-1848 Paris exile. Their movement for Irish freedom attracted the support of the poorer classes in Ireland and immigrant proletarians in Britain and America. Charles Kickham, perhaps the most talented Fenian journalist and author of a number of influential agrarian novels, mainly *Knocknagow*, had a deep understanding of the grievances of Irish tenant farmers and agricultural laborers. Still people like Stephens, O'Mahoney and Kickham were convinced that the advocacy of social reform would split the Republican movement and antagonize potential Protestant recruits.
21. The quote is from a statement by Cornelius Lucy, bishop of Cork, justifying clerical guidance in the political arena. After many Irish nationalists, including Dail politicians, rejected the implications of this pretentious claim, Lucy clarified his original position. He said that while the church interprets divine law and has the right to instruct laymen on moral questions, it does not have the sanctions to enforce compliance to its teachings. He also emphasized that the church's power "extends only to the religious and moral implications of what goes on", and that she "has no competence to control

9

On occasion necessity demanded that Irish nationalism enlist the passions of the rural masses by agitating the land question. Although tenant rights and Land League rhetoric and tactics were radical, the final result, peasant proprietorship, was extremely conservative. Land owning Irish peasants, like their brethren throughout the world, tend to resist change. As citizens of the Free State and Republic, they joined the priests and shopkeepers as champions of a chauvinistic, narrow minded nationalism designed to isolate Ireland from the contaminations of the modern world. Clerical spokesmen for the troika used the contents of Irish cultural nationalism to justify isolationism.

Since the Young Ireland movement in the 1840s, cultural nationalists have criticized the Catholic influence in Irish nationalism, but their message unwittingly has aided the advance of clerical power. In their effort to de-Angelicize Ireland they attacked British values. They portrayed the Irish as spiritual people finding beauty in the things of nature. In contrast, Englishmen were coarse materialists. Industrialism was a cruel monster devouring the human spirit. Urbanization corrupted men's personalities. Utilitarianism was a vulgar justification of avarice. Without the presence of the British and their perverse culture, Ireland would be a rural paradise. Catholic spokesmen exploited the cultural nationalist attack on British materialism, twisting the hope for a unique, intellectual, Irish Ireland into a demand for a unique, holy, Catholic Ireland. Cultural nationalists warned against the shallow, alien values of West Britonism; the priests and their friends sermonized against pornographic books, lewd movies, licentious dance halls and the evils of socialism. Irish Catholicism contained the worst of two worlds: the sexual obsessions of Anglo-Saxon Protestantism and the intellectual bankruptcy and authoritarianism of Latin Catholicism.

If the marriage between Irish and Catholic has made it difficult for nationalism to develop social and economic ideas and programs essential to the needs of modern society, it has also limited the response of the church to the challenges of the contemporary world. Changes in theological opinion, interpretations of the moral law and liturgy go down much better in Catholic communities where religious and ethnic identities are divorced or vague. In Ireland, however, innovations in religious thought and practice challenge a nationality still associated in many minds with Catholic pietism.[22] The reluctance of the Catholic church in Ireland to respond to the spirit of Vatican II reflects a conservatism that is lay as well as clerical.

But life patterns are changing in Ireland. Industrialization and urbanization; travel and tourism; the impact of the communication media—television, cinema,

public affairs itself or indicate the practical ways and means of dealing with current problems.'' Lucy reminded Catholics that the ''church no more supersedes the individual conscience in public life than it does in private life'' (John Whyte, *Church and State in Modern Ireland*, p. 313). Of course in Ireland the church broadly defines the religious and moral implications of political conduct, and, as Sean O'Faolain has pointed out, in a country where the people believe that the sacraments are essential for salvation, spiritual weapons can be more powerful than legal or political ones (*The Bell*, June 1951). In a country ninety-five percent Catholic, almost all practicing, the church can exert more influence on the public consciences of the politicians than on the private consciences of ordinary citizens.

22. Pietism and puritanism are accepted characteristics of modern Irish Catholicism, but Emmet Larkin in ''The Devotional Revolution in Ireland,'' *The American Historical Review* 77 (June 1972):625-652, has established that both were products of a post-famine Romanization movement sponsored by Paul Cardinal Cullen. *The Changing Face of Catholic Ireland*, ed. by Desmond Fennell, (London, 1968), supports Larkin's thesis and emphasizes the impact of British and American Protestant values in the development of an Irish Catholic puritanism.

radio and the printed word; influences from a more liberal spirit in northern European Catholicism; the decision to join the Common Market: all these encourage intellectual vitality and curiosity, even in theology and moral philosophy, and increase demands for a higher standard of living and a more interesting life style. New attitudes challenge the position and authority of the Catholic church. In a public referendum, many Irishmen, perhaps a majority, would vote to abolish restrictions on divorce and birth control. They might even demand a lower clerical profile in the field of education. If there is not a majority for such reforms at present there probably will be in the near future. A new generation of Irish Catholics in the South would like to expand the areas open to the decisions of private conscience and prove to Protestants in the North that they would have nothing to fear in a United Ireland. In time Ireland will reconcile her laws and institutions to the values of liberal democratic nationalism. But Ireland will remain culturally Catholic. Four centuries of history have left her with no other choice.

THE ORIGINS AND CHARACTER
OF IRISH-AMERICAN NATIONALISM

Thomas N. Brown

The Origins and Character of Irish-American Nationalism

by Thomas N. Brown

One in name and one in fame,
The sea-divided Gael.[1]

THE IRISH have always been proud of their ability to assimilate their conquerors, who often, like the Burkes and Geraldines, became *hibernis ipsis hiberniores*. No doubt the charm of Ireland explains this phenomenon as well as the boast of John O'Leary that one had but to live in Ireland six years and he was Ireland's.[2] But why should the immigrant who abandoned the old country and his son who never saw it become in many ways more Irish than the Irish themselves? What was there in the immigrant experience that transformed the indifferent peasant into a fierce and aggressive Irish nationalist? What was the character of this nationalism that shifted the balance of Irish political power, so that in 1885 the London *Times* could say with confidence that "the Irish Question is mainly an Irish-American question?"[3]

Lecky and Froude thought the immigrant's hatred for England derived from their bitter memories of the Famine.[4] And undoubtedly that terrible tragedy added to the immigrant's sense of wrong, determining many of them to achieve freedom for Ireland so that that horror could not be repeated.[5] But the peasantry in Ireland, who had directly borne the Famine, were largely unmoved by the revolutionary movements that excited the immigrant. The peasantry looked back to the days that were gone rather than forward in hopes for an independent Ireland; not until another

---

[1] Thomas D'Arcy McGee, "Salutation to the Celts," *The Poems of Thomas D'Arcy McGee* (New York, 1886), 135.

[2] Quoted in Kathleen Hoagland, *A Thousand Years of Irish Poetry* (New York, 1951), xlii.

[3] Quoted in Boston *Pilot*, January 2, 1886.

[4] W. E. H. Lecky, *Leaders of Public Opinion in Ireland* (New York, 1903), II, 184; James Anthony Froude, "Romanism and the Irish Race in the United States," *North American Review*, CXXX (1880), 39.

[5] See F. Hugh O'Donnell, "Fenianism—Past and Present," *Contemporary Review*, XXXIII (1883), 753; John F. Maguire, *The Irish in America* (New York, 1868), 692-697. See letter of M. Carroll, *Irish World*, December 25, 1875 and another from "Castleblaney," *ibid.*, March 30, 1876.

327

famine threatened in 1879 did they join the nationalists. The Famine clearances, as one Irishman observed, "had sown dragon's teeth from the Hudson to the Mississippi."[6] If this phenomenon was more apparent here than in the land of the Shannon, it was because of the peculiar experience of the Irish in America.

Over three million Irish came to the United States in the years between 1845, the first year of the Famine, and the death of Charles Stuart Parnell in 1891.[7] The immigrant tide ebbed and flowed according to the push and pull of conditions in Ireland and America. It was at flood in 1851, when more than 221,000 entered and lowest in the depression year of 1877, when less than 15,000 came over. Munster and Connacht suffered the greatest losses, but the North and the rich land of Leinster were stripped as well.[8] The youngest and healthiest of Ireland's laborers, and farmers got out; pushed off the land by cattle, they saw that Ireland offered them little and America a great deal.[9] "The wheat pulled up," a friend of Thomas Davis lamented in the dark year of 1847, "and the tares left."[10]

The immigrants landed in America like tired migratory birds. Prisoners of their own poverty, they were confined to the cities in which they landed or to those of the interior, on rivers and railways, where work was available. The potato culture of Ireland had not prepared them for the hard ways of the frontier farm, nor given them the skills to work the land the Yankees left behind.[11] Gregariousness led later immigrants to adhere to the pattern of urban settlement. In 1890, when the number of Irish-born in the

---

[6] A. M. Sullivan, *New Ireland* (Philadelphia, 1878), 335.

[7] United States Bureau of the Census, *Historical Statistics of the United States, 1789-1945* (Washington, D. C., 1949), 33-34.

[8] Stanley C. Johnson, *A History of Emigration from the United Kingdom to North America, 1763-1912* (London, 1912), Table VIII, 351; Eric Strauss, *Irish Nationalism and British Democracy* (New York, 1951), 138; L. Paul-Dubois, *Contemporary Ireland* (Dublin, 1911), 355.

[9] *Report From the Select Committee on Tenure and Improvement of Land (Ireland) Act . . .* (House of Commons, 1865), 122; G. Locker-Lampson, *A Consideration of the State of Ireland in the Nineteenth Century* (London, 1907), 276; Strauss, *op. cit.*, 138.

[10] Charles Gavan Duffy, *Four Years of Irish History* (London, 1883), 448.

[11] See Oscar Handlin, *Boston's Immigrants . . .* (Cambridge, Mass., 1941), 64; Mary Gilbert Kelly, *Catholic Immigrant Colonization Projects in the United States, 1815-1860* (New York, 1939), 267 ff.; Henry J. Browne, "Archbishop Hughes and Western Colonization," *The Catholic Historical Review,* XXXVI (1950-1951), 257-285. For a detailed study of Irish settlement in a rural state see M. Judith McDonald, *A History of the Irish in Wisconsin* (Washington, 1954).

United States was highest, less than 15 per cent were engaged in agriculture; the remainder were bunched in the great cities, with 190,418 in New York, 71,441 in Boston and 70,028 in Chicago.[12]

Everywhere the Irish performed the crude labor of the factory, construction gang and mine; the women, when fortunate, worked as servants in homes of the wealthy. The Irish were the "hewers of wood and the drawers of water," as they had been at home. In many ways life in the New World was as harsh as that in the Old. Rents were high, the fear of eviction everpresent[13] and wages were often only enough for subsistence. The tenements of Boston's Fort Hill, New York's Five Points and Chicago's Bridgeport were as unhealthy as the wretched huts of Ireland. By the 1890's, many sons and grandsons of immigrants had risen into the ranks of the middle class. But the recent arrival and his family perpetuated the tradition that a great portion of America's poor be of Irish blood.[14]

The Irish were the exploited and proscribed poor; used but not accepted by the Protestant majority. And economic exploitation was a harder irony to bear in America because it occurred within the forms of civil and religious liberty.[15] Moreover, America taught the Irish that poverty was not a necessary condition of existence. The squalor of Ireland infuriated Irish-Americans as it never had the peasant Irish.[16] And their own poverty they laid upon the conscience of England.[17]

------

[12] See the *Eleventh Census: 1890*, Part I (Washington, D. C., 1895), Table I, 670 and Part II (Washington, D. C., 1897), cxlvi, cxlix. The figure given is actually 15.51 per cent, but includes those engaged in agriculture, fisheries and mining. Only 11.60 per cent of the males were engaged solely in agriculture.

[13] Robert Ernst, *Immigrant Life in New York City, 1825-1863* (New York, 1949), 50.

[14] For the condition of the Irish before the Civil War see Handlin, *op. cit.*, 59-127; Ernst, *op. cit.*, 48-83; Bessie L. Pierce, *A History of Chicago* (New York, 1940), II, 13, 151-153. For the post-Civil War period see Fred A. Bushee, *Ethnic Factors in the Population of Boston* (New York, 1903), 27 ff. and Robert A. Woods, ed., *The City Wilderness* . . . (Boston, 1898), *passim*.

[15] See letter of "J. S.," *Irish World*, September 18, 1875 and another from "D. A. Q.," Boston *Pilot*, February 16, 1878.

[16] See letter of Jennie F. Byrnes, Boston *Pilot*, August 19, 1882. See also John Mitchel, *The Crusade of the Period and Last Conquest of Ireland (Perhaps)* (New York, 1873), 212-213; Frances Morehouse, "Irish Migration of the 'Forties'," *American Historical Review*, XXXIII (1927-1928), 586.

[17] See *Irish World*, June 24, 1876 and letters of "C. D. G.," *ibid.*, October 26, 1878, "Ballaghaslane Beara," *ibid.*, January 1, 1876; E. L. Godkin, "An American View of Ireland," *Nineteenth Century*, XII (1882), 180.

The Irish were also the most homesick of all immigrants; their songs and poems, equalling in pathos those of the Negro, became a part of America's folk literature. The very isolation of their lives in Ireland intensified the anguish felt when separated from old scenes and faces. To quiet the pangs of loneliness and to meet the problems of American life the immigrants grouped together. Despite the suspicions of nativists, who believed them divisive, the organizations formed were natural and healthy,[18] reflecting the pluralism of American society and the divisions within the Irish-American community, for Irish societies expressed class as well as group consciousness. The wealthier Irish in Boston could join the Charitable Irish Society, those in New York and Philadelphia the Friendly Sons of St. Patrick, while the corner saloon and the neighborhood clubs served for the poor.[19] Many early Irish militia companies were recruited exclusively from workers of particular skilled trades; and among the most effective organizations were those dedicated exclusively to the economic welfare of their members.[20]

But loneliness also evoked in the immigrant mind an image of Ireland that cut through the divisions natural to the immigrants in America. Batt O'Connor, an immigrant bricklayer, whom a St. Patrick's Day parade in Providence, Rhode Island, helped convert to revolutionary nationalism, said that "to leave Ireland does not make one love Ireland more, but it does make one aware of the strength of that love."[21] Since his arrival in 1893, O'Connor had been lonely in America: "I would try to recall the smell of the turf, and I would think of the streams in which I went fishing, and the places where I found a bird's nest. . . ." Ballybeyond could not easily be recaptured, but longing for it brought Irishmen together and from their meeting came a new awareness of love for Ireland: "I walked in that procession [the Providence Parade] and in the emotion I felt, walking as one of that vast crowd of Irish emigrants celebrating our national festival, I awoke to the full consciousness of my love for my country."

---

18 Ernst, *op. cit.*, 182-183.
19 Handlin, *op. cit.*, 160; Ernst, *op. cit.*, 126; Mary Alphonse Frawley, *Patrick Donahoe* (Washington, D. C., 1946), 105.
20 Handlin, *op. cit.*, 164; Ernst, *op. cit.*, 125-126, 128.
21 Batt O'Connor, *With Michael Collins in the Fight for Irish Independence* (London, 1929), 14.

Irish-American nationalism was thus in part a symptom of the immigrant's homesickness; the immigrant agitator was not a swindler or filibuster, but "that much more unreasonable animal, a dreamer."[22]   Nevertheless, the immigrant's nationalism was too fierce an enthusiasm to derive simply from the passivity of a nostalgia for the Old Country.   Indeed, it was the ruling passion for many of the second and third generation who knew only America. Like the almost mythic Captain William Mackey Lomasney, who was born in Ohio and blown to bits by his own dynamite under London Bridge in 1883, the fiercest nationalists were often the sons of immigrants.[23]

Patrick Ford, who was born in Galway in 1837 and came to America when he was eight, during the first year of the Famine, is a reliable witness of the experiences that made him the most influential American advocate of Irish freedom in the second half of the nineteenth century.   To a reporter from the *Pall Mall Gazette,* he admitted that as a youth in Boston he knew nothing of Ireland.   "I might as well have been born in Boston. . . .   I brought nothing with me from Ireland—nothing tangible to make me what I am."[24]   Young Patrick Ford walked the streets of Boston during the years when the Know Nothings controlled the state of Massachusetts and anti-Irish feeling was strong everywhere. Day after day he sought work only to see the signs reading "no Irish need apply" that were the insulting barriers which separated the Irish from the American community.

---

[22] John White, *Sketches From America* (London, 1870), 369. See also the comments of James Stephens, the Irish Fenian, on the loneliness of John O'Mahoney, the American Fenian, in the "American Diary of James Stephens, 1858-1860," *Report of the Deputy Keeper of the Records for the Years 1938-1945.* Government of Northern Ireland (Belfast, n.d.), 32.

[23] For Lomasney, see Mark F. Ryan, *Fenian Memories,* T. F. O'Sullivan, ed. (Dublin, 1945), 117-120; William O'Brien *Recollections* (London, 1905), 74-78; T. P. O'Connor, *Memoirs of an Old Parliamentarian* (London, 1929), 216. Also born in Ohio and equally fierce was Captain John McCafferty, who planned a raid on Chester Castle in 1867 and later sought to capture the Prince of Wales. See William O'Brien and Desmond Ryan, edd., *Devoy's Post Bag* (Dublin, 1948), I, 37, 67-68. Cited hereafter as *Devoy's Post Bag.* Parnell believed the second generation were the most useful to the Irish cause in America. See his speech at Galway, October 24, 1880, *Irish World,* November 20, 1880. This was the opinion of A. M. Sullivan, "Why Send More Irish Out of Ireland," *Nineteenth Century,* XIV (1883), 141. The *Irish Nation* (New York), August 18, 1883, edited by the exile, Devoy, disagreed. See, however, the letters of M. Carroll and T. Cale Foster in *Irish World,* December 28, 1875 and December 8, 1877.

[24] Reprinted in *Irish World,* September 25, 1886.

> I went seeking in this way for some months . . . finding constantly that the fact that I was Irish and a Catholic against me. I was not yet awake about Ireland, but I began to think early, to read whatever I could lay hands on . . . and to think over what I had read.

Under the pressure of Know-Nothingism, young Ford came to the conclusion that he was the victim of the "conditions of poverty and enslavement" which gripped the land of his birth; and decided that "it was necessary for everyone of Irish blood to do all in his power to change that state of things."[25]

The Know-Nothing movement made the immigrant aware that he was despised and that the lines separating him from the Protestant Ascendancy (his term) were more sharply drawn than in Ireland,[26] where generations of personal relationships had blurred them over. The battle lines were first clearly drawn during the 1840's when the Irish had achieved sufficient political power to threaten institutions long cherished by the Protestant majority, as in New York and Philadelphia, or to frustrate hopes for social reform, as in Boston.[27] In the conflict which raged during the 1840's and 1850's the composition of the immigrant community was shaped. Many of the Protestant Irish joined the Know-Nothings, as did some non-Irish Catholics. But the latter were engulfed by the immigrant wave and Catholic and Irish became identified. The passive Church of the gentle Bishop Cheverus gave way to the militant Church of Archbishop Hughes.[28] When Orestes' Brownson, anxious to preserve the earlier Anglo-American character of the Catholic Church in America, attempted criticism

---

[25] *Ibid.* For similar experiences see Michael P. Curran, *The Life of Patrick A. Collins* (Boston, 1906), 8 ff.; Frawley, *op. cit.,* 13, 21, 45 ff.; letter of Thomas Craven, Boston *Pilot,* January 2, 1886 and *ibid.,* August 3, 1878, December 6, 1884.

[26] See E. L. Godkin's opinion in Rollo Ogden, ed., *Life and Letters of E. L. Godkin* (New York, 1907), I, 181-184; also Thomas Colley Grattan, *Civilized America* (Second Edition, London, 1859), II 8; Philip H. Bagenal, *The American Irish* . . . (Boston, 1882), 129; White, *op. cit.,* 353-354; William Dillon, *The Life of John Mitchel* (London, 1888), II, 53; Michael Buckley, *Diary of a Tour in America,* Kate Buckley, ed., (Dublin, 1886), 142.

[27] Handlin, *op. cit.,* 197 ff.; Ernst, *op. cit.,* 168 ff.; Ray Allen Billington, *The Protestant Crusade, 1800-1860* (New York, 1936), 193.

[28] Thomas T. McAvoy, "The Formation of the Catholic Minority in the United States, 1825-1860," *The Review of Politics,* X (1948), 25 ff. *Celts and Saxons, Nativism and Naturalization: A Complete Refutation of the Nativism of Dr. Orestes Brownson by the Catholic Press of the United States* (Boston, 1854), 10.

of the Irish immigrant, he found that for the majority of the hierarchy and for the Catholic press defense of the Irish was the greater imperative.[29] It was natural then for Patrick Ford to see nativism as primarily an expression of hatred for the Irish-Catholic poor and it was not unreasonable for him to conclude that the germ of the immigrant's predicament lay in Ireland.

Irish-American nationalism then had its origins in loneliness, poverty and prejudice. Compressed into ghettos, the Irish used their numbers and the group consciousness which the ghetto fostered to nourish, as nativists complained, "their foreign feelings and their foreign nationality."[30] Within the Irish-American community old allegiances were reflected in the Kerry villages and Donegal squares found in all the great cities. Nevertheless, the immigrants realized that in a hostile land their Irishness mattered more than their provincial differences. Life in America, said Patrick Ford, lifted the Irishman out of "the littleness of countyism into the broad feeling of nationalism."[31]

Rooted in the immigrant's experience, this nationalism was peculiarly Irish-American, reflecting his compulsive sense of inferiority, his sensitiveness to criticism and his yearning for respectability. For the immigrants, as their first historian said, paid too high a price "for butcher's meat and glazed shoddy instead of honest frieze,"[32] and were badly in need of America's esteem. Stage Irishmen learned to their surprise that jokes which evoked laughter in Dublin drew hisses in New York. Dion Boucicault, the prolific Irish playwright, had his play the *Shaughraun,* based on a popular Irish folk tale, mobbed in Boston.[33] The stage Irishman was too much like the stereotype believed in by nativists and indeed was often too close to the truth of the immigrant situation to be accepted

---

[29] *Celts and Saxon, passim;* McAvoy, "Catholic Minority," *loc. cit.,* 29-30.
[30] Samuel F. B. Morse, *Imminent Dangers to the Free Institutions of the United States* . . . (New Edition, New York, 1854), Appendix 30, 23-29, in Edith Abbott, ed., *Historical Aspects of the Immigration Problem: Selected Documents* (Chicago, 1926), 448.
[31] *Irish World,* December 17, 1881; Stephen J. Brown, "The Question of Irish Nationality," *Studies* (Dublin), I, (1912), 635. See also O'Donovan Rossa, "Skirmisher's Column," *Irish World,* May 6, 1876.
[32] Thomas D'Arcy McGee, *The Irish Position in British and Republican North America* (Montreal, 1866), 17.
[33] For the experiences of Barney Williams, Harrigan and Hart and Boucicault see Boston *Pilot,* May 4, 1878, January 5, 1884; *Irish World,* February 8, 1873, October 2, 1875, May 6, 1876, March 13, 1877, January 5, 1878, March 2, 9, 1878.

by the sensitive. Michael Davitt, the most compelling Irishman of
his generation, reveals in a speech, given before a large audience at
Cooper Union in 1880, how the soft spot in immigrant psychology
served the interests of Irish nationalism:

> You want to be honored among the elements that constitute this
> nation, as a people not coming from a paupered land; and in
> order that no sneers be cast on you when you stand for any
> position . . . you want to be regarded with the respect due you,
> that you may be thus looked on, aid us in Ireland to remove the
> stain of degradation from your birth and the Irish race here in
> America will get the respect you deserve.[34]

This appeal was a commonplace of Irish nationalist oratory
and immigrant responsiveness to it involved the United States in
the latter half of the nineteenth century in many an embarrassing
situation abroad and often snarled domestic politics in the thicket
of Anglo-Irish relations. A United States court in 1856 warned
the Irish Emigrant Aid Society of Cincinnati, a revolutionary body
led by Michael Doheny, the Forty Eighter, that there "can be no
such thing as a divided allegiance."[35] In the years before the
Irish-American community was moulded under the impact of
Know-Nothingism there had not been such a problem. The Irishman, whether Catholic or Protestant, was not then cut off from
the main stream of American life.

When the United Irishman, Thomas Adis Emmet, came to the
United States in 1803, he found that his "principles and his suf-
ferings" opened the most fashionable doors in New York to him.[36]
His career and that of his friend and fellow rebel, Dr. William Mac-
Neven, were brilliant and happy; and like those of other prominent
Irishmen of the period were essentially American, not Irish-Ameri-

---

[34] *Irish World*, November 13, 1880. For other expressions of this popular
theme see speech of T. F. Meagher at Cooper Institute, January, 1864, in
Michael Cavanagh, *Memoirs of General Thomas Francis Meagher* . . . (Worcester, Mass., 1892), 358; T. O'Neill Russell, *Irish Nation*, June 11, 1882;
Irish World, March 18, 1876; letters from "American Born Irishman," "Sen-
tinel," "Tipperary Man" (to O'Donovan Rossa), *ibid.*, March 25, 1876, February 29, 1876, February 16, 1878; lecture of P. K. Walsh to Irish Literary
Association of Cleveland, *ibid.*, April 8, 1876; "W. M. C." column, *ibid.*, July
22, 1876; speech of T. C. Luby at Ogden's Grove, Chicago, *ibid.*, August 31,
1878; speech of William Connolly at Wendell's Assembly Rooms, New York
City, *ibid.*, November 13, 1880.
[35] Extract from *United States vs. Samuel Lumsden et al.* (1856), (*Bond's
Reports*, I, 9-27), quoted in Abbott, ed., *op. cit.*, 483.
[36] R. R. Madden, *The United Irishmen, Their Lives and Times* (Third
Series, Second Edition, London, 1860), III, 157.

can.[37]   The poor, ragged immigrants of post-Famine years were
men of another sort.   Neither their principle nor their proletarian
character commended them to America.[38]   They could not reply
to sneers about their foreign birth with an answer like Emmet's
to William Pinkney "that he was Mr. Pinkney's equal in birth, in
rank and in connexions."[39]   Unlike Emmet and MacNeven, out-
standing Irishmen in the latter half of the century, whether busi-
nessmen like William Onahan, or politicians like Patrick Collins,
depended for their influence upon the ability to exploit the sentiments of the Irish-American community.[40]

It is true that the Irish in America always revealed some interest
in the affairs of their native land; but in the early years of the
nineteenth century this did not distinguish them from native Americans.   The increase in the 1840's of evangelical fervor to spread
democracy must have brought many Americans into the branches
of O'Connell's Repeal society, which were organized in Richmond,
Savannah, and elsewhere where the Irish population was slight.[41]
Those who tried to persuade James Gordon Bennett to join the
Repeal society of New York assured him that the "great movement
of Repeal in Ireland . . . was only the beginning of a grand revolutionary drama, that soon would be able to subvert the monarchies
and aristocracies of England, France and all western Europe. . . ."[42]
Most of the delegates to the Repeal convention which met in New
York City in the fall of 1843 had Irish names, but many did not.
That Robert Tyler, the son of the President, headed the Convention was perhaps less important than the fact that Richard Johnson
and Lewis Cass, as well as the Whigs, Horace Greeley and William
Seward were among those who thought action to restore self-
government to Ireland was a legitimate interest of a citizen of

---

[37] For the careers of Emmet and MacNeven see Madden, *op. cit.*, III, 141-
196; Deasmunhan O Raghallaigh, "William James Macneven," *Studies*, XXX
(1941), 247-259; Thomas Addis Emmet, *Memoir of Thomas Addis and Robert
Emmet* (New York, 1915), I, 391 ff.
[38] Handlin, *op. cit.*, 129 ff.
[39] Madden, *op. cit.*, III, 152.
[40] See Curran, *op. cit.*, for Collins and for a timid evaluation of Onahan
see M. Sevina Pahorezki, *The Social and Political Activities of William James
Onahan* (Washington, D. C., 1942). See also, McGee, *Irish Position,* 7.
[41] See the *Freeman's Journal and Catholic Register* (New York), July 22,
September 21, 1843.
[42] New York *Freeman's Journal,* September 30, 1843; Don C. Seitz, *The
James Gordon Bennetts . . .* (Indianapolis, 1928), 114.

the United States;[43] and this at a time when denouncing the immigrant paid greater political dividends than twisting the lion's tail.

From the collapse of the Repeal agitation, however, until Parnell and Gladstone joined hands in 1886 responsible native Americans generally refused to participate in American societies designed to further Irish freedom. Their reluctance was not due, as one English propagandist suggested,[44] to loss of sympathy as a result of experience with the troublesome Irish, but rather to changes in character and orientation of Irish-American national societies. However much American supporters of Repeal may have been entranced by the possibility of democratic revolutions going off like fused dynamite throughout Europe, they had preferred to dwell on its peaceful aspects and constitutional purposes.[45] But after the arrival of the Forty Eighters Irish national societies here, no matter how euphemistically named and ostensibly peaceful their purposes, were controlled in varying degrees by revolutionists. As John Mitchel discovered, Americans, despite their sympathy, were disinclined to embarrass their own country by backing revolution in Ireland.[46]

A more important influence in persuading native Americans to remain aloof from Irish societies was the heavy cloud of hate and fear that hung over them, the bitter heritage of the Know-Nothing conflict. When the thunderheads of Civil War lowered in 1861, the immigrants, as Professor Hansen has said,[47] were flung upward to positions in field and factory that they could not have aspired to during the preceding years. Nevertheless, they did not lose their sense of group consciousness. Spokesmen for the Irish remained extremely sensitive to discrimination in the army,[48]

---

[43] *Freeman's Journal*, July 22, September 2, 30, 1843; T. D. McGee, *A History of the Irish Settlers in North America* . . . (Boston, 1851), 133. William H. Seward, *An Oration on the Death of Daniel O'Connell* (Buffalo, 1855), 5, 35.

[44] Sir Lepel Griffin, "The Harvest of Democracy," *Fortnightly Review*, XLI (1884), 387. The Louisville *Courier Journal*, aware that Americans no longer participated in Irish affairs as they had during O'Connell's period, thought increased wealth in America had diluted interest in struggling nationalities. See *Irish Nation*, May 10, 1883.

[45] See the account of a Repeal meeting at Cincinnati in *Freeman's Journal*, July 22, 1843.

[46] Dillon, *op. cit.*, II, 38-39.

[47] Marcus Lee Hansen, "The Second Colonization of New England," *New England Quarterly*, II (1929), 553.

[48] R. G. Athern, *Thomas Francis Meagher* . . . (Boulder, Colorado, 1949), pp. 99, 122.

and the Draft Riots of 1863 demonstrated that the Irish poor retained their sense of grievance.[49] In that famous occasion at the Rappahanock when Irish soldiers in both blue and gray joined their voices across the battlefield in singing the immigrant lament, "Deep in Canadian Wood," they expressed the powerful emotional ties which held them together in a nation torn by war.[50] Those who did not share in this emotional legacy of Irish-America could only have been uncomfortable in the societies that it produced.

It is true that Irish-American nationalism was as much an affair of the spirit, a state of mind, as it was a matter of birth or religion.[51] One did not have to be Irish to love Cathleen na Houlihan. Nor did one have to be an Irish-American to share in his ideals. What was needed was to feel his special grievance, the injustice of being alien. In England and America Irish nationalism was largely the cause of the poor—those, according to the *Irish World,* who felt "heavily the shame of the disgraced condition to which our race is reduced. . . ."[52] Except in cities like San Francisco, where the Irish bore no social stigma, the wealthier Catholic Irish ("lace-curtain Irish") kept themselves aloof from the organizations of the poor.[53] And the Protestant Irish found it necessary to describe themselves as Scotch-Irish in order that they be distinguished from the peasant poor.[54] On the other hand, Americans like Wendell Phillips and James Redpath, who had ridden the tide of pre-Civil War reform and were marooned when it ebbed, found a natural place as champions of Irish-America in the years of the Great Barbecue.[55]

---

[49] Basil Lee, *Discontent in New York City, 1861-1865* (Washington, D. C., 1943), 105 says that it was "not the Irish as Irish who revolted but the penniless Irish worker. . . ." It was, however, their poverty that gave the Irish their intense sense of group consciousness.

[50] O'Donnell, "Fenianism," *loc. cit.,* 751.

[51] On this aspect of nationalism see W. B. Pillsbury, *The Psychology of Nationality and Internationalism* (New York, 1919), 267.

[52] *Irish World,* May 27, 1876. See also "An Occasional Correspondent," *ibid.,* December 18, 1875, February 10, 1877 for the role of rich and poor in Irish Nationalism in England.

[53] Boston *Pilot,* May 22, 1880, November 11, 1882; *Irish World,* December 4, 1875, May 20, 1876; Charles Lord Russell of Killowen, *Diary of a Visit to the United States of America,* C. G. Herbermann, ed. (New York, 1910), 144-145; Thomas Beer, *The Mauve Decade* (New York, 1941), 127-128.

[54] See Samuel Swett Green, *The Scotch-Irish in America* (Worcester, Massachusetts, 1895), especially 7, 9, 51-52, 56, 59. Also the Wilmington, Delaware, *Herald* quoted in *Irish World,* February 10, 1877; Boston *Pilot,* April 27, 1878; T. O'Neill Russell, *Irish Nation,* May 27, 1882; White, *op. cit.,* 360.

[55] James Redpath, former abolitionist and biographer of John Brown, after

Nevertheless, Wendell Phillips and James Redpath were exceptions. Americans not of Irish origin only rarely involved themselves in the nationalist affairs of the immigrant in the years preceding the alliance of Parnell with Gladstone. This isolation from the American community intensified the immigrant's problem of divided loyalties. At once more American than the Americans[56] and more Irish than the Irish, the immigrant, in the phrase of the sociologist, Robert Park, was the "marginal man,"[57] astride two worlds. The task of his leaders was so to interpret his experience that the tensions created by this ambivalence might be resolved. Loyalty to Ireland had to be reconciled with loyalty to America.

William MacNeven suggested the proper approach to the problem when he stated in his *Pieces of Irish History,* alluding to the American Revolution and Irish resistance to British rule, that "What was tyranny against the American would necessarily be tyranny against the Irish; and the resistance so glorious in one country could not be accounted a crime in the other."[58]   He spoke, however, only in defense of the revolutionary enterprises of the United Irishmen. Later leaders were to link the fate of Ireland to America in a broader stream of history. Most significant were the lectures given by Thomas D'Arcy McGee, another Forty Eighter. Beginning with the possible discovery of America by St. Brendan, according to an interpretation of an old legend, McGee catalogued the names of Irishmen prominent in the colonial

suffering a nervous breakdown in 1879, was sent to Ireland in 1880, at the height of the land agitation, as a correspondent for the New York *Herald Tribune.* Very quickly he became one of the most effective propagandists of the Irish Land League. And in his dispatches and many lectures in Ireland and America he identified the Irish movement as a continuation of the old abolitionist effort to extend the rights of men. In 1882 he established *Redpath's Weekly* as an organ of Irish land reform. See F. Horner, *The Life of James Redpath* (New York, 1926), 255-261 and James Redpath, *Talks About Ireland* (New York, 1881), bound in D. P. Conyngham, *Ireland Past and Present* . . . (New York, 1884). Because of his age Phillips was less active than Redpath when the Irish Question came forward in the late 1870's, but he spoke often on the question in Boston and his speech on Daniel O'Connell in 1875 was one of his best efforts. His hostility to respectable Boston opinion and his sympathy for the working classes made him welcome in the Irish camp, where he found the old libertarian spirit of the 1850's. See Roche, *op. cit.,* 142, 153, 217, 228, 236; Van Wyck Brooks, *New England Indian Summer* (New York, 1940), 120, 331; T. A. Devyr, *Irish World,* May 20, 1876.

[56] See Lady Wilde, Boston *Pilot,* May 24, 1879; John Lancaster Spalding, "Mr. Froude's Historical Method," *North American Review,* CXXX (1880), 287; "Diary of an Amateur Emigrant," Boston *Pilot,* September 26, 1885.

[57] See Everett V. Stonequist, *The Marginal Man* . . . (New York, 1937), 1-9; 83-106, 159 ff.

[58] William J. MacNeven, *Pieces of Irish History* . . . (New York, 1807), iii.

and early national periods of America.   Lacking the brilliant insights into the situation of the immigrant often found in his other works, the lectures adequately demonstrated that the Irish were not new to America.[59]   When told to go home to Ireland if he did not like the treatment received in America, the Irishman could use McGee's facts to answer: "This is our country. We bought it dearly. We like it well and we intend to stay in it."[60]   America belonged to the Irish as much as anyone.

McGee did not originate this form of apologetics,[61] but he was the first to give it such wide currency.   Later enthusiasts, stirred by the possibilities of the argument, ransacked libraries for more information and gave their imagination freer rein.   William R. Grace and Honest John Kelly embellished the lectures of McGee to the delight of audiences in the 1880's.[62]   In a later series of lectures McGee had said that at the dawn of American history there were three Catholic figures: a lady, a sailor and a monk.[63] His successors would have it that there was also an Irishman; as indeed they insisted there was at every important turn in America's development.   St. Brendan, in their opinion, was the undoubted discoverer of the New World;[64] and the glory of the Irish was further enhanced by the knowledge that an Irishman accompanied the Admiral of the Ocean Sea on his first voyage.   This latter information proved, according to the Boston *Pilot,* "that the Irish is no bastard or corrupt stock, but one of the seminal races of the earth. . . ."[65]   And as befitted such a race its soldiers were virtually responsible for winning the American Revolution against a vicious horde of English and German Protestants;[66] and its blood was to

[59] McGee, *History of the Irish Settlers in North America, passim.*

[60] *Irish World,* January 8, 1876. See also Spalding, "Mr. Froude's Historical Method," *loc. cit.,* 287 ff.

[61] See "Hibernicus," *What Brings so Many Irish to America* (New York, 1845).

[62] William R. Grace, *The Irish in America* (Chicago, 1886); John Kelly, *The History of the Early Irish Settlers in America* (New York, 1884).

[63] T. D. McGee, *The Catholic History of North America* (Boston, 1855), 17.

[64] *Irish World,* September 21, 1872, March 22, 1873; Conyngham, *op. cit.,* 161.

[65] Boston *Pilot,* June 8, June 22, 1878; Conyngham, *op. cit.,* 161.

[66] *Irish World,* September 21, 1872, March 18, 1876, August 19, 1876; Boston *Pilot,* February 11, 1885, September 10, December 10, 1887, August 17, 1889.   See also the controversy between Duffield Osborne and Thomas F. Meehan, "Irish Aid in the American Revolution," *North American Review,* CXXXXV (1888), 97-99, 319-324.

be found in the veins of innumerable famous Americans, even
in the nativist veins of Samuel Morse.[67]

In his compulsive love for Ireland the immigrant was only
intensifying his Americanism, for Ireland struggled for democracy.
"The cause of America in 1776 is the cause of Ireland in 1876."[68]
England was the enemy of both and in a curious way continued to
oppress America. Not only was the corrupt Irishman of America's
cities a direct product of English rule,[69] but the money he sent
home to Ireland was a tax levied upon America. The United States
in the 1880's, said James Redpath, voicing the argument of many,
in this way suffered the very injustice of taxation without representation that had sparked the American Revolution.[70]

This glorious confusion of fact with fancy was neither descrip-
tive of the immigrants' true situation, nor of their ambitions. They
had not simply dedicated themselves as American democrats to
the spread of that faith in Ireland, where indeed it was held at
a discount by many nationalists. But McGee's system of apologetics did help to bridge over one gap which yawned beneath the
immigrants as "marginal men," giving them a dramatic sense of
participation in the greatness of America, while ignoring the
massive squalor under which they lived. And this must have
nourished egos suffering from painful feelings of inferiority.

The immigrants, of course, realized that they did not voice
influential American opinion; that the Irish national struggle did
not join Ireland and America, but rather the discontented and
depressed of both countries. Armed with this insight, they employed another argument—one closely entwined with that from
history but even more imaginative and grand—that derived from
their view of themselves as Celts. The sea-divided Gaels were
bound together by the ties of race; and these all men must respect.
The trans-Atlantic allegiance worked to the benefit of America,
for one of the Celt's special missions was to protect the Declaration
of Independence against "derogation by the Anglo-Saxon Ascendancy."[71] The struggle for human freedom, which bound the

---

[67] *Irish World*, March 22, 1873, *ibid.*, July 15, 1876; Conyngham, *op. cit.*, 162-167.

[68] *Irish World*, January 22, 1876.

[69] James J. Clancy, *Ireland: As She Is, Has Been and As She Ought to Be* (New York, 1877), 10.

[70] *Irish World*, December 18, 1880; also Boston *Pilot*, January 3, 1879.

[71] *Irish World*, September 28, 1872.

destinies of Ireland and America was in truth an aspect of the epic struggle of the Celt against the Saxon.

Modern awareness of the Celt is not much older than the publication in 1765 of MacPherson's *Ossian*, which made the melancholy Celt of the young Scot's imagination a familiar figure to the reading public of Goethe's Europe.[72] MacPherson's "translations" began a long literary war over the question of their authenticity and, as a by-product, another over the character of the ancient Celts, stimulating Irish antiquarians to defend as well as to discover their country's past. This work was carried on largely under the patronage of the Ascendancy and did not dispose the antiquarian toward hostility to England. Charlotte Brooke, whose *Reliques of Irish Poetry* served to refute many of the Celt's detractors, presented her study in the hope that it would improve Anglo-Irish relations.[73]

But Celtic studies pursued by members of the middle class, anxious as many were for reform, did stimulate antagonism to the Saxon. Charlotte Elizabeth Phelan, interested in using Gaelic as an instrument of Protestant proselytizing, confessed that her studies converted her from being a "dangerous Orangewoman" into "something like a rebel."[74] Some ten years later Thomas Davis deliberately fostered this tendency with his writings in the *Nation*. Then for the first time the Celtic past became a factor in modern Irish politics.[75] Though Gavan Duffy believed that Davis had succeeded only in making converts to antiquarianism,[76] his

---

[72] Eoin MacNeill, *Phases of Irish History* (Dublin, 1919), 4-9; Magnus MacLean, *The Literature of the Celt* . . . (London, 1902), 252, 370. See also Alfred Nutt's introduction, Matthew Arnold, *The Study of Celtic Literature* (London, 1910), xxi.

[73] Charlotte Brooke, *Reliques of Irish Poetry* . . . (Dublin, 1879), vii. See Edward O'Reilly's preface to *Transactions of the Iberno-Celtic Society for 1820*, I, Part I (Dublin, 1820) for the antiquarian societies before 1820.

[74] See Hugh Anderson, *The Life and Letters of Christopher Anderson* (Edinburgh, 1854), 145. Charlotte Elizabeth Phelan, well known as a writer of stories for Protestant children, lived in Ireland from 1819 to 1824. Anderson, a Scotch Baptist, founded the Irish Society in 1818 for the purpose of converting the Gaelic speaking Catholics. See also Christopher Anderson, *The Native Irish and Their Descendants* (Third edition, London, 1846).

[75] Davis and others in 1845 founded the Celtic society, which in 1853 became the Ossianic Society; both were more intensely Irish than the earlier antiquarian societies. Desmond Ryan, *The Sword of Light* (London, 1939), 179 ff. Compare for example, the nationalist spirit of John O'Mahoney's comments in his translation from the Gaelic of Geoffrey Keating, *The History of Ireland* . . . (New York, 1857), 7 with the dedication of Owen Connellan, *A Practical Grammar of the Irish Language* (Dublin, 1844).

[76] Charles Gavan Duffy, *Thomas Davis* (London, 1890), 93, 352-353.

pseudonym "The Celt" became one of the important symbols of militant Irish nationalism in the last half of the nineteenth century. A symbol that soon found employment in America.[77]

The Know-Nothing conflict had generated self-consciousness among native Americans, leading them to explore their Anglo-Saxon origins and to assert the moral superiority of that race over "the untaught and wretched Celt."[78] In the years following the Civil War the arrogance of the Anglo-Saxon myth-makers increased as Darwinian thought appeared to give scientific validity to their claims.[79] In response, the Irish, emboldened by their increasing economic and political status, elaborated a Celtic interpretation of history. Lacking historians and publicists of the caliber of Edward Augustus Freeman, James Anthony Froude, or even Goldwyn Smith, second only to Froude in denigrating the Celt, the Irish were forced to rely upon the standard works of Irish apologetics,[80] and the scholarly if difficult studies of Eugene O'Curry, John O'Donovan and W. K. Sullivan.[81] They drew also upon such eccentric enthusiasts as Martin O'Brennan, who believed the language of the Celts had been the speech of the Garden of Eden.[82] The backhanded compliments of Matthew Arnold and the findings of Zeuss and other continental philologists were available to them in that disorganized collection of other men's ideas which Father Ulick Bourke, of St. Jarlath's College, Connacht, published as *The Aryan Origins of the Gaelic Race and Language* (1876).[83]

---

[77] See Nutt's introduction, Arnold, *op. cit.*, xii-xiii. See also the prospectus, "The Map of Our Journey," *The Celt* (Kilkenny), I (1857-1858), 1-4. This weekly was founded in August, 1857, by disciples of Davis. Seven years earlier Thomas D'Arcy McGee, who had learned about the Celts in the British Museum, had founded *The American Celt* in Boston. For the latter see Josephine Phelan, *The Ardent Exile* (Toronto, 1951), 22-23, 102.

[78] E. E. Hale, *Letters on Irish Emigration* (Boston, 1852), 47-58, quoted in Abbott, ed., *op. cit.*, 461. See also Handlin, *op. cit.*, 214.

[79] Edward N. Saveth, *American Historians and European Immigrants, 1875-1925* (New York, 1948), 15.

[80] Works such as John Lynch, *Cambrensis Eversus*, Matthew Kelly, ed. (Dublin, 1848); Matthew Carey, *Vindicae Hibernicae* (Philadelphia, 1819), and MacNeven, *Pieces of Irish History*.

[81] Especially O'Curry, *Lectures on the Manuscript Materials of Ancient Irish History* (Dublin, 1861).

[82] See letter of O'Brennan in *Irish World*, February 23, 1878; and *ibid.*, January 20, 1877. For his life see Boston *Pilot*, February 23, 1878. His works include *Ancient Ireland* . . . (Dublin, 1855) and O'Brennan's *Antiquities* (Dublin, 1858).

[83] For enthusiastic reception of Bourke's book see *Irish World*, December 7, 1878, January 5, 1878; Boston *Pilot*, April 27, 1878.

The American Celts had little use for the dreamy ineffectual race of Arnold's *Study of Celtic Literature*. The virtues they found in their race were typically American. Not magic but the ability to assimilate and fuse together disparate racial groups they believed to be the special genius of the Gael,[84] whose ancient society erred only in being too democratic.[85] Though they agreed with Arnold that the Celt was less materialistic than the Saxon,[86] they generally claimed for their race the very achievements that Freeman and his American counterpart, Herbert Baxter Adams reserved for the Germanic peoples.[87] The origins of democratic institutions, which these historians traced back to the "tun" of the dark German forests, the philo-celts found on the sunny slopes of Tara. Representative government, trial by jury, popular education were among the gifts tendered the modern world by the Celts of Ireland.[88]

The American Irish were aware that they were insisting upon Celtic particularism at a time when philologists were asserting a common Aryan origin for Saxon and Celt.[89] There was a certain embarrassment also in the fact that some of the most ancient Gaelic names belonged to members of the anti-nationalist Irish gentry, while Celtic partisans bore names obviously Saxon or Norman in origin.[90] Nevertheless, the Celtic myth served as a useful defensive weapon at a time when prevailing American opinion had it that America in its people and institutions was essentially Anglo-Saxon. So long as this view prevailed the Irish were prepared to claim America for the Celts; to insist that the foundations of America rested on the Blarney stone, not on Plymouth Rock.[91]

---

[84] See James O'Leary, *Ireland Among the Nations* (New York, 1874), 197; letter of T. F. Galwey, Boston *Pilot*, May 30, 1885. For Arnold's understanding of the Celt see John V. Kelleher, "Matthew Arnold and the Celtic Revival," in Harry Levin, ed., *Perspectives of Criticism* (Cambridge, Massachusetts, 1950).

[85] Clancy, *op. cit.*, 14-141; O'Mahoney, trans., Keating, *op. cit.*, lii; T. N. Burke, *Ireland's Case Stated* . . . (New York, 1873), 26; *Irish World*, October 9, 1875.

[86] Bishop Keane, "The Future of the Celt," Boston *Pilot*, November 24, 1885; Justin McCarthy, *ibid.*, August 18, 1885; *ibid.*, June 14, 1890.

[87] Saveth, *op. cit.*, 16ff.

[88] Clancy, *op. cit.*, 119, 133-134; "European Correspondent," *Irish World*, October 9, 1875; Boston *Pilot*, July 14, 1888.

[89] Bourke, *Aryan Origins of the Gaelic Race*, 116-117.

[90] *Irish Nation*, January 6, 1883; Bourke, *Aryan Origins of the Gaelic Race*, 171 ff.

[91] *Irish World*, August 19, 1876, August 10, 1878, January 6, 1877; Boston *Pilot*, October 8, 1881; April 9, 1887; *Irish Nation*, April 22, 1882.

Defenders of the Celt organized Philo-Celtic societies throughout America for the revival of the Irish language, which had some influence upon the language revival in Ireland, preceding by four years the foundation in 1876 of the Dublin Society for the Preservation of the Irish Language. In 1873 the first of the Philo-Celtic societies was begun in Boston.[92] By 1878 there were five societies in New York and in the following year branch societies were in existence in over thirteen American and Canadian cities, from Boston to San Francisco. And the study of Gaelic was reported to be a favorite recreation among soldiers in the forts of the frontier.[93]

Father Ulick Bourke was impressed by the phenomenon of immigrants in America learning there the language they had the "misfortune not to have learned at home."[94] But these were few. In America as in Ireland the mass of the Irish were ashamed of or had no use for the old tongue. Even the Philo-Celtic clubs as it turned out were less interested in the language than they were in disproving Froude's statement, made during his lecture tour in 1870, that the "Irish as a nation have done nothing which posterity will not be anxious to forget."[95] When T. O'Neill Russell of the Dublin language society came to the United States in 1878, he found the Irish-American press indifferent and even opposed to his efforts to revive the language. The *Irish World,* whose enthusiasm for Gaelic had influenced Dubliners as well as immigrants, warned the hopeful Russell that it had taken up the language movement in 1871 only to prove to "educated dunces" that Ireland had a glorious literature in her native language.[96] The Land League soon proved more exciting than Irish grammar, robbing the Philo-Celtic societies of members and their quarrels over

---

[92] See letter of "Philo-Celt," *Irish World,* September 25, 1875; *ibid.,* August 31, 1878; Robert E. Park, *The Immigrant Press and Its Control* (New York, 1922), 50. On Dublin language society see Ryan, *Sword of Light,* 211 ff.

[93] Boston *Pilot,* November 30, 1878, January 11, 1879; *Irish Nation,* June 30, 1883.

[94] Bourke, *Aryan Origins of the Irish Race,* 103. See also letter of Bourke, *Irish World,* April 28, 1877.

[95] *Irish World,* October 9, 1875. Also letter of P. J. Daly, *ibid.,* April 15, 1876; Proceedings of Boston Philo-Celtic Society in *ibid.,* September 18, 1875, and letters discussing wisdom of reviving Irish in *ibid.,* February 8, 1872, September 28, 1872, March 15, March 22, 1873.

[96] August 31, 1878; also *ibid.,* July 1, 1876.

whether Roman or Irish type should be used further weakened these organizations.[97]

Ten years after its founding the Boston Philo-Celtic society reframed its constitution in order that new members might join without committing themselves to the labor of studying Gaelic. The society continued to insist, however, that the "cultivation of the Irish or Celtic language and the publication of Irish or Celtic literature," was the only way to "vindicate the character of the Irish as a race, from the foul slanders heaped upon them for centuries by English or Anglo-Saxon writers. . . ."[98]

The American Irish used the symbol of the Celt, as had Davis, to disarm their detractors and to give their people hope by giving them pride in the past. But they used it also to provide Irishmen, no matter how far removed in time and place from Ireland, with a rationale for nationalist action and to justify such action before their critics.[99] They bent history to their will, but better scholars in the camp of the enemy were as guilty with less reason.

The principal instrument of instruction in Celticism and in the dogmas of nationalism was the Irish-American press. Newspapers in Ireland were largely irrelevant to the fixed life of the peasantry, but to the uprooted Irish of America they were almost a necessity. The paper brought the news of home, of ship sailings and arrivals; it offered correspondence columns to locate lost relatives and others to locate jobs. It taught the peasant the customs and manners of bourgeois America and was his champion in a hostile society. All newspapers devoted to the immigrant taught some brand of nationalism, if for no other reason than that it aided circulation. It was to the newspapers that the immigrant turned when in his newly awakened consciousness he sought knowledge of the Irish and of Ireland.[100]

---

[97] See *Irish Nation*, December 4, 1881, May 13, 1882, May 27, 1882, June 11, 1882, April 27, 1883; *Irish World*, June 15, 1878, April 5, 1879, May 3, 1879; Boston *Pilot*, April 19, 1879. The question of the type to be used also bedeviled the movement in Ireland. See *Irish Nation*, March 24, 1883; the Chicago *Citizen*, August 24, 31, 1889; Ryan, *Sword of Light*, 214 ff.

[98] *Irish Nation*, April 15, 1882.

[99] See T. P. O'Connor, Boston *Pilot*, October 22, 1881; A. M. Sullivan, *ibid.*, January 6, 1883; *ibid.*, May 26, 1883, November 5, 1887; *Irish Nation*, December 31, 1881; letter of F. McGowan, *Irish World*, March 4, 1876.

[100] See, for example, "Answers to Correspondents," *Irish World*, September 4, 11, 18, 1875, for immigrants seeking the origins of their Gaelic names and information about Irish history. See "Hints for Household," *ibid.*, July 12,

Not until the 1840's was the newspaper assured a stable place in immigrant culture. Catholic newspapers, fed by the increasing anti-Irish feeling of the 1830's, served the immigrant, but efforts to establish purely secular Irish newspapers had failed.[101] The immigrant flood of the 1840's, especially that after the Famine, provided the Irish press with readers and the Know-Nothing movement gave it a cause. The defeat of Young Ireland at Ballingarry made writers available. Thomas D'Arcy McGee, John Mitchel, T. F. Meagher, Michael Doheny and John O'Mahony were among those who tried their hand at teaching nationalism by means of the immigrant press in the 1850's. Mitchel's *Citizen*, begun in New York in 1854, boasted a circulation of 50,000 within a few months.[102]

The identification of Irish with Catholic, with Archbishop Hughes the exalted defender of both, was simple enough to maintain during the years when the Liberator strode the boards. But the advent of Young Ireland introduced new factors. To Archbishop Hughes, as to his friend Cardinal Cullen, the young refugees reeked with the smell of Mazzini. "Political confectioners," Hughes called them in his best style, "who seal up the poison of their infidelity in sugar plums of flattery to popular prejudices. . . . They are not of those Irishmen who have preserved the nationality and honor of their country by preserving their faith in the midst of persecution."[103] Aroused by McGee's "strong doses of patriotism," administered in his *Nation* and later by Mitchel's attack upon the temporal claims of the Papacy, the Archbishop verbally smashed the *Nation* and then John Mitchel's *Citizen* and helped to drive their editors out of New York.[104]

That Irish nationalism was not to be identified with Catholicism was apparent in the varying ways cleric and nationalist approached the Celtic myth. For the priest, Irish history was a

---

1879, for instruction to the female readers on how to prepare food, clean carpets and keep kitchens neat. See also article on Andrew Johnson, *ibid.*, September 11, 1875, illustrating how one could rise through self-education and "if he be patient, persevering, upright, self-reliant, temperate, and frugal he must succeed."

[101] A. W. Baumgartner, *Catholic Journalism . . .* (New York, 1931), 12 ff.; Handlin, *op. cit.*, 178 ff.; Frawley, *op. cit.*, 37 ff.; Ernst, *op. cit.*, 150-153.

[102] Dillon, *Mitchel*, II, 50.

[103] John R. G. Hassard, *Life of the Most Reverend John Hughes . . .* (New York, 1866), 311.

[104] Dillon, *Mitchel*, II, 5-51 *passim;* Phelan, *op. cit.*, 92-99.

religious drama, a long martyrdom of a people naturally Christian that was permitted by God in order to spread His Word.[105] Aware of the pleasant irony that the immigrant Irish were carrying Catholicism everywhere throughout the English speaking world, churchmen saw in that tattered figure an arm of the Lord and in the Famine which sent him forth the mysterious "logic of God."[106] Nationalists furiously rejected this fatalism; and argued persuasively that Catholic England had been as destructive of the liberties of the Irish as was Protestant England.[107] Daniel O'Connell, of course, was the hero of the Catholic Celtophile. Nationalists remembered his surrender at Clontarf and believed his political doctrines had corrupted the Irish people.[108] Nationalists were also convinced that clerics thought of Ireland as a pawn that could be sacrificed whenever the diplomacy of restoring England to the Faith demanded.[109]

When John Mitchel was attacked, as he said, by "Archbishop Philo-Veritas," on the one hand and by a "true-blue Orangeman" on the other,[110] he defined by implication the road nationalists in America would have to travel. Similar though it was to that followed by their brethren in Ireland, it had fewer stones. The American Irish, having acquired the aggressiveness of their new country, were less submissive to the clergy than the Irish at

---

[105] The best of these interpretations is August J. Thebaud, *Ireland: Past and Present* . . . (New York, 1878), especially 60-105. See also James O'Leary, *Ireland Among the Nations*, 138 ff.

[106] J. C. Curtin, *The Lectures, Sermons, Addresses and Letters of Dr. D. W. Cahill* (New York, 1885), 120. See also Thebaud, *op. cit.*, 414; J. L. Spalding, *The Irish People and Catholic Colonization* (New York, 1880), 33-63. Archbishop Hughes, however, at the height of the Famine declared that not God but the British government was responsible. See his *A Lecture on the Antecedent Causes of the Irish Famine in 1847*. (New York, 1847).

[107] See James G. McGuire, *Ireland and the Pope* . . . (San Francisco, 1888), 32; *Irish World*, March 18, 1876, December 8, 1877; John P. Sutton, *ibid.*, March 16, 1878; Michael Davitt in Boston *Pilot*, August 14, 1880; John O'Leary, *Recollections of Fenians and Fenianism* (London, 1906), II, 31; O'Donovan Rossa, *Recollections, 1838-1898* . . . (New York, 1898), 110.

[108] See Maguire, *Ireland and the Pope*, 13 ff.; Boston *Pilot*, January 17, 1880, August 21, 1880, January 8, 1881, March 5, 1881, March 18, 1882; *Irish World*, March 18, 1876, July 28, 1877.

[109] See *Irish World*, September 18, 1875; P. K. W., *ibid.*, October 2, 1875; "Transatlantic," *ibid.*, November 6, 1875; *ibid.*, January 15, 1876; "Transatlantic," *ibid.*, February 26, 1876; *ibid.*, January 22, 1876, February 5, 1876; *United Irishman* (Liverpool) in *ibid.*, February 26, 1876; *ibid.*, April 8, 1876, May 13, 1876, August 5, 1876, March 3, 1877; "Transatlantic," *ibid.*, June 9, 16, 1877; P. K. Walsh to Rossa, *ibid.*, October 13, 1877; *ibid.*, February 16, 1878, September 11, 1878, November 2, 1878; Boston *Pilot*, August 21, 1880.

[110] Dillon, *op. cit.*, II, 62; Phelan, *op. cit.*, 99; Hassard, *op. cit.*, 311.

home.[111] Moreover, with the decline of Know-Nothingism the clergy lost their place as spokesmen for the Irish in public affairs. Even in the 1850's the most popular historical defense of the immigrant was not that of Archbishop Hughes, but those lectures of his enemy, Thomas D'Arcy McGee. The Archbishop's personal influence remained until his death, but shortly afterwards the fire-like spread of Fenianism demonstrated how weak was the control of the priest in Irish affairs. And no churchman in after years was able to wield the power of Archbishop Hughes.[112]

Politicians, reformers and nationalists took over the leadership of the depressed Irish, guiding them often into uncharted waters, too murky and dangerous for the Church. Opposition to those excursions by the hierarchy, however wise and foresighted, gave verisimilitude to the charge of some that the Church blocked the path of the Irish poor. Few nationalists, however, wanted a break with the Church. They understood its influence in Ireland and the faith of the Irish in America. And the majority of the American hierarchy in the last half of the century, fearing to weaken that faith by unwise opposition and often themselves in sympathy with Irish aspirations, were more cautious than their counterparts in Ireland in challenging the nationalists.[113] Sharing to some extent each other's faith, but responsive to different allegiances, the churchman and the nationalist lived in a state of uneasy tension.

The decline of clerical influence in secular affairs and the development of a national body of readers (most major Irish papers had national circulations) rendered the press independent of the local bishop. New York was the chief center of Irish-American publishing in the 1880's, with five weeklies designed for Irish

---

[111] See White, *op. cit.*, 352; Lady Wilde, Boston *Pilot*, May 24, 1879; "Diary of an Amateur Emigrant," *ibid.*, September 26, 1885; Justin McCarthy, *ibid.*, April 18, 1885.

[112] Spalding, *op. cit.*, 147. For the Catholic hierarchy after the Civil War see Thomas T. McAvoy, "The American Catholic Minority in the Latter Half of the Nineteenth Century," *Review of Politics*, XV (1953), 281-288.

[113] See Bishop John A. Luers, Fort Wayne, Indiana, to Archbishop John B. Purcell, March 23, 1864; Bishop Amadeus Rappe, Cleveland, Ohio, to Archbishop John B. Purcell, September 13, 1866; Archbishop John B. Purcell, Cincinnati, Ohio, to Cardinal Barnabo, September 16, 1870; Bishop William McCloskey, Louisville, Kentucky, to Archbishop John B. Purcell, April 25, 1871. The Cincinnati Papers, University of Notre Dame. See also Fergus MacDonald, *The Catholic Church and Secret Societies in the United States* (New York, 1946), 34-37.

consumption; but every important center of Irish population supported at least one newspaper.[114]   The *Irish World*, founded in 1870 by the messianic Patrick Ford, driven to advocate almost every kind of social radicalism during the bad times after 1873, fought many battles with the clergy and was barred from at least two dioceses,[115] but it remained during the 1870's and 1880's the most popular Irish-American paper in the country.[116]   Having for readers the same class whom Joseph Pulitzer would try to reach in the next decade, the *Irish World* anticipated the techniques of Yellow Journalism.   Sensational headlines and drawings (tearful Erin crouching in terror over her unstrung harp under the blooded whip of John Bull) enlivened the front page.   Ford specialized in collecting money for Irish causes and the thrill of seeing one's name in print as a contributor perhaps aided circulation.

But Ford was also a serious moral reformer.   The abolition of slavery, temperance, social reform, Irish national freedom had at one time or another commanded his energies.   Like William Lloyd Garrison, on whose *Liberator* he had learned the printer's trade, he was rigidly righteous and his language was thick with the Old Testament.   His paper, studded with complex speculations on subjects ranging from usury to theology, was witness to the earnestness of himself and his readers.   He also possessed a deep capacity for self-deception and the *Irish World* was able to shift from radical, even revolutionary criticism of capitalism in 1878 to

---

114 They were the *Freeman's Journal*, the *Tablet*, the *Irish World*, the *Irish Nation* and the *Irish American*.   The *Western Watchman* of St. Louis, the Chicago *Citizen* and the *Northwestern Chronicle* of St. Paul, Minnesota were among the important papers in the Midwest.   Influential also was the Irish Catholic Benevolent Union *Journal* of Philadelphia.   For the last named see Joan M. Donohoe, *The Irish Catholic Benevolent Union* (Washington, D. C., 1953).

115 In 1879 the paper was condemned by Bishop Baltes of the Alton (Illinois) diocese and by Bishop Gilmour of Cleveland.   See *Irish World*, March 15, 22, April 5, 12, 1879.   See also the paper's controversy with a Brooklyn priest in *ibid.*, March 30, 1878, and letter of "J. C." on the matter, *ibid.*, April 13, 1878.   The quarrels grew out of the paper's attacks upon "the priest in politics" and out of fear of its radical democratic teachings.

116 N. W. Ayer, *American Newspaper Annual* . . . (Philadelphia, 1885), 66, gives the *Irish World's* publishing report, which claims a circulation of 80,000.   Edward Alden, *American Newspaper Catalogue* . . . (Cincinnati, 1882), credits the paper with a circulation of 100,000.   Ford in 1879 distributed a special issue of 1,500,000 copies.   *Irish World*, January 18, March 29, 1879.   For the influence of the paper see Russell, *op. cit.*, 191 and M. F. McGowan in *Irish World*, March 4, 1876.

the advocacy of Harrison ten years later without losing its sense of moral rectitude.[117]

Next in influence to the *Irish World* during the Parnellite period was the Boston *Pilot*,[118] whose shrewd realism, under the brilliant editorship of John Boyle O'Reilly, was in sharp contrast to the quarrelsome evangelicism of Ford's paper. A man of fine literary gifts and great personal charm, O'Reilly was disposed by character and experience towards moderation. Born in Ireland in 1844 and at the age of twenty-two sentenced to imprisonment for participating in the Fenian conspiracy, the *Pilot* editor very early knew the limitations of revolutionary organizations.[119] Though he remained the confidant of the revolutionaries and was prepared to support their projects, his own energies were expended in ways more in keeping with his talents. Ten years after a romantic escape from an Australian prison colony, O'Reilly was firmly established as owner and editor of the *Pilot,* oldest and most respected of immigrant papers, and as a fully accredited member of Boston's literary community.[120]

More than anyone else, O'Reilly understood the function of the leader in an immigrant group. Each week the *Pilot* taught the displaced peasants the disciplines of toleration and fair play necessary in a multi-racial society, thereby earning the applause of Brahmin Boston.[121] But he was also the champion of the Irish whenever they were (or thought they were) under attack. And he never hesitated to use their considerable political power in the interests of Irish-America. The ambiguity of O'Reilly's public behavior (often denying by action what he affirmed in editorials, novels, and poems) and his limitations as a liberal reformer derived from his role as immigrant leader. For the advance of Irish-America depended upon the solidarity of its members and the

---

[117] See *Dictionary of American Biography* (New York, 1937), VI, 518; *Irish World*, April 14, 1877.

[118] Ayer, *op. cit.*, 31 lists the circulation of the *Pilot* at 70,000. Alden, *op. cit.*, 121 in 1883 lists the ciriculation at 67,300.

[119] See James J. Roche, *The Life of John Boyle O'Reilly* (New York, 1891), 1-47, 107-116; O'Reilly, Boston, to O'Donovan Rossa, March 2, 1872. John Boyle O'Reilly papers, Irish Collection, Boston College. O'Reilly, Boston, to John Devoy, January 28, 1871. Devoy's *Post Bag*, I, 13-14.

[120] See letter of Oliver Wendell Holmes, Boston, to O'Reilly, October 2, 1876. Mary Boyle O'Reilly papers, Boston Public Library; Brooks, *op. cit.*, 311-312, 412; Robert Grant, *Fourscore . . .* (Boston, 1934), 168-172; Roche, *op. cit.*, 153-154.

[121] Brooks, *op. cit.*, 311-312; Beer, *op. cit.*, 118.

impregnability of its fortress. If pursuit of reform divided the immigrant community, the effort was abandoned and the divisions were denied. The *Pilot* was ever alert to assaults from without and always insisted that all was serene within the fortress.[122]

In his concern for the New Ireland O'Reilly did not forget the old. "We can do more good by our Americanism than by our Irishism,"[123] he said, believing that in this way American public opinion might be transformed into a powerful moral force that would pressure England to grant Irish demands. This Yankee version of O'Connell's strategy was not, of course, original with the editor of the *Pilot,* nor practiced exclusively by him. But more than anyone else O'Reilly kept constantly in mind that Ireland had to plead her cause in the market place of America; and grateful Irishmen in later years ascribed the policy to him.[124]

If Patrick Ford was essentially the American reformer, not really Irish at all, then John Devoy, editor and founder of the *Irish Nation* from 1881 until it failed in 1886, was preeminently the political refugee abroad; the Irish revolutionary virtually untouched by American experience. Imprisoned as a Fenian in 1867, he came to America upon his release three years later; and against the advice of his friend John Boyle O'Reilly stepped immediately into the turbulent waters of Irish revolutionary politics in New York city.[125] Until his death in 1928 he was the chief guardian of Cathleen ni Houlihan in America, protecting her from the radicalism of the Fords and the compromises of the O'Reillys.[126] Though not unaware of the urgency of the need for social reform

---

[122] For a different interpretation of O'Reilly's career see Arthur Mann, *Yankee Reformers in the Urban Age* (Cambridge, Mass., 1954), 24-51. Mr. Mann believes that it was the "Catholic part of his Irish background" that accounts for the contradictions of O'Reilly's career. No doubt conservative Catholic pressures did inhibit O'Reilly's actions. See for example the letter of S. G. Kelly, Boston, no date, to Henry George. Henry George Collection, New York Public Library. But had O'Reilly not believed so intensely in the need for Irish-American unity he might have followed Patrick Ford and others in more radical and divisive action.

[123] Quoted in R. H. Lord, J. E. Sexton and E. T. Harrington, *History of the Archdiocese of Boston* (Boston, 1944), III, 396. See also Roche, *op. cit.,* 207, 208, 231; Boston *Pilot,* July 23, 1870, March 12, 1871.

[124] See *Speech of the Honorable Michael Davitt, M. P., Delivered Before the First National Convention of the United Irish League of America,* Faneuil Hall, Boston . . . October 20, 21, 1902 (n.p., n.d.).

[125] See letter of O'Reilly, Boston, Massachusetts, to Devoy, 1871, in *Devoy's Post Bag,* I, 43-44.

[126] See Desmond Ryan, *The Phoenix Flame* (London, 1937), for a popular study of Devoy's career.

in Ireland, Devoy would not permit it to slow the quest for national freedom. But in his hands the work of preparing a revolution lost its romance and became a grubby business. It was a principle of John O'Leary's that there were some things a man must not do to save his country.[127] Unencumbered by O'Leary's temperament, Devoy used every strategy and weapon available to him. Perhaps because it was too purely Irish, like its editor, the *Irish Nation* never attained great popularity, but because it represented the considered opinions of a formidable body of revolutionists its influence was not to be measured by circulation.[128]

That the Irish-American press met the needs of the immigrants' peculiar situation was demonstrated by its survival and growth even during the depression years of the 1870's. In the Celtic myth and the promise of nationalism the press gave heroic meaning to the experience of the uprooted. But the immigrants were heirs of O'Connell, as well as of Thomas Davis, and too utilitarian to permit their dreams to become an obsession. While Ireland year by year became more luxuriously green in their memories, they turned to the techniques of organization which Daniel O'Connell had taught them. Collective action, they believed, would win Irish national freedom and thus the respect of Americans; and would also advance their material interests in this country. "We need," said the *Irish Nation*, "a permanent organization of the Irish race in America that will not alone look to the needs of Ireland, but to the defense of Irish interests here."[129]

Many organizations were designed to uplift the Irish. The Catholic Total Abstinence Union professed to accomplish this by the cult of sobriety. Its banner, according to the "hymn" of the Union would fly over a "nation freed from bondage and a race redeemed from shame."[130] The Irish Catholic Benevolent Union, the Ancient Order of Hibernians and the Irish sections within the Knights of Labor had similar ambitions.[131] All of these

---

[127] See William Butler Yeats, *The Autobiography of William Butler Yeats* (New York, 1938), 183.

[128] Alden, *op. cit.*, lists the circulation of the *Nation* in 1883 as 10,000.

[129] *Irish Nation*, January 6, 1883. See also A. M. Sullivan, Boston *Pilot*, January 6, 1883; *Irish Nation*, December 31, 1881; *Irish World*, October 26, 1878.

[130] Quoted in James J. Green, "Organization of the Catholic Total Abstinence Union," American Catholic Historical Society *Records*, LXI (1950), 85. See also *Irish World*, June 24, 1876.

[131] Terence Powderly was in 1882 an executive of the Irish Land League

subscribed to the dogmas of nationalism and possessed a stability and wealth that the more volatile nationalist organization could not ordinarily command. But their very immersion in the practical problems of the immigrant narrowed their membership and, by stirring up the dusts of class and sectional division, inhibited their capacity for leadership of the Irish-American community.

Inevitably, the Abstinence Union had a limited appeal; when it included mutual aid among its attractions, it met competition from other benevolent organizations and the liquor interests were always powerful enemies.[132] The Hibernians had been discredited in the 1870's by their connections with the labor terrorism of the Molly Maguires in Pennsylvania.[133] The founders of the I.C.B.U. hoped for a grand alliance of Irishmen, but in trying to lure the immigrant from labor unions, the organization bucked a too powerful tide.[134]

Perhaps the most grandiose plan conceived for the salvation of the immigrant was that of the Irish Catholic Colonization Society of America (1878-1891), a bold effort to relocate the slum dwellers on the prairies of the West. It had some success when, as in the colonizing work of Archbishop Ireland of Minnesota, it operated in aid of the normal pattern of land settlement, helping those who already had the money, skills and desire for farming the West.[135] But the larger hopes of breaking the grip of the cities upon the Irish poor were not fulfilled. Vested interests were opposed, and the mass of the Irish were apathetic, preferring with most Americans of these years the bright lights of the cities.[136] Ironically, during the disappointing life of the Colonization society, the immi-

---

of America, Senior Guardian of Clan na Gael Camp 470 as well as head of the Knights of Labor. He was unusual only in his leadership; others shared these interests. See Frank Bannon, New York City, to Powderly, March 12, 1882; John J. Joyce, New York City, to Powderly, April 20, May 21, 1882. Powderly papers, Catholic University of America. See also Powderly's speech before the Land League at Buffalo, *Irish World*, March 19, 1881; "Ballaghaslane Beara," *Irish World*, December 20, 1875.

[132] Green, *loc. cit.*, 94 ff.; *Irish World*, January 29, 1876.

[133] MacDonald, *op. cit.*, 109 ff.; John O'Dea, *History of the Ancient Order of Hibernians and Ladies Auxiliary* (Philadelphia, 1923), III, 1046-1048.

[134] Aaron I. Abell, "The Catholic Factor in Urban Welfare, 1850-1885," *The Review of Politics*, XIV (1952), 319.

[135] See Abell, *loc. cit.*, 321; M. E. Henthorne, *The Irish Catholic Colonization Association of the United States* (Champaign, Illinois, 1932), 74; Spalding, *op. cit.*, 179-180.

[136] Henthorne, *ibid.*, 65, 71 ff.; Abell, *loc. cit.*, 323.

grants, nationally organized in the Land League, contributed hundreds of thousands of dollars to make the peasant of Ireland
proprietor of the land he worked. "Our people," lamented one
enthusiast for colonization, "would be more willing to give five
dollars a day to buy a faded green flag with a tarnished sunburst
than one dollar for an acre of land."[137]   Only by transcending
their situation in America, only by fixing on goals sufficiently
removed from their American anxieties, could Irish-Americans
achieve the solidarity that was their dream. This was the special
function of the Irish nationalist organization, of which the first
significant one was the Fenian Brotherhood.

A struggling revolutionary body, when begun in 1858, like so
many others in that decade, the Brotherhood's membership
increased enormously under the stimulus of the Civil War. The
name Fenian derived from the Fianna, that ancient warrior band
whose exploits under Fionn MacCumhail make up the second
cycle of Irish mythology, and is testimony to the lonely romanticism
of John O'Mahoney, Young Ireland exile and founder of the organization in America.[138]   The sister organization in Ireland, led by
that artful conspirator, James Stephens, preferred the less mystical
name of the Irish Revolutionary Brotherhood. Though the Irish
body was insignificant compared to the American, Stephens insisted
upon running both as a dictator until O'Mahoney, responsive to
conditions in America, refashioned his group along democratic
lines. Anxious to conform to American neutrality laws, as well
as to demands here for democratic procedures, and fearing also
clerical condemnation as a secret society, the Fenians, in their
first national convention in 1863, made the "Head Center" an
elective official providing him with a cabinet, also elected by
the assembly delegates.[139]   They affirmed that the society was
neither illegal, nor secret, and, convinced that a war between England and the United States, which would effect their "deliverance,"
was imminent, they made clear the American nature of their con-
cerns: "We say our deliverance, for the privilege of living among

---

[137] The Reverend Thomas A. Butler, "Open Council" column, *Irish World,*
August 10, 1878.
[138] See John Savage, *Fenian Heroes and Martyrs* (Boston, 1868), 110 ff.;
Stephens, "Diary," *loc. cit.,* 32.
[139] William D'Arcy, *The Fenian Movement in the United States, 1858-1886*
(Washington, D. C., 1947), 33-38.

a free people . . . but makes us feel the more keenly the suffering and degradations of our old land."[140]

War, however, did not come and members of the Brotherhood, anxious to precipitate action, forced further reorganization upon O'Mahoney. At the Philadelphia Convention in 1865, with six-hundred delegates present, the office of Head Center was abolished and that of a President to be elected by the General Congress of the Fenian Brotherhood was substituted. Congress, made up of a Senate and House of Delegates, was invested with all legislative powers. Members of the individual Fenian circles throughout the country elected the Delegates who in turn, in Congress assembled, elected members to the more august assemblage of the Senate. Power to originate all money bills was given to the Senate and theirs too was the responsibility to approve all cabinet appointments. The President of that body was also Vice-President of the Brotherhood.[141] With the Constitution of the United States as a model, and the procedure of its Congress as an ideal, the Fenians, as one of them later wrote, formed "a distinct Republic within the American Republic."[142] From their capitol in the old Moffat mansion (opposite Union Square, New York City), which flew the Fenian flag of the harp and sunburst, they raised an army, issued letters of marque and reprisal, negotiated with the United States and otherwise conducted themselves as an important power.[143]

Having separated their governmental powers in approved American fashion, the Fenians then fell into bickering between the legislative and executive branches which the system fosters. A few months after the Philadelphia convention, the Senate deposed O'Mahoney as President for exceeding his constitutional authority, thus displaying the same yeasty arrogance that set the Senate of the United States in this same year plotting against Andrew Johnson. O'Mahoney, however, refused to retire as chief of the Fenians and organized his own body that did away with the elaborate paraphernalia of government fabricated at Philadelphia.[144] "Cut

---

[140] Chicago *Tribune* (Saturday), November 7, 1863.

[141] D'Arcy, *op. cit.*, 79-81.

[142] Savage, *op. cit.*, 56-57, 66. See also *Seventh National Congress, F. B.: Proceedings of the Senate and House of Representatives of the Fenian Brotherhood in Joint Convention* . . . (New York, 1868).

[143] D'Arcy, *op. cit.*, 74, 81, 85.

[144] D'Arcy, *op. cit.*, 103-108.

and hack the rotten branches around you without pity,"[145] O'Mahoney was advised by Stephens, who, like many other Irish revolutionists, disliked the Americanization of the movement by the Senate wing.[146] Nevertheless that body, led by William R. Roberts, a wealthy New York dry goods merchant, of consummate ability in composing flamboyant denunciations of the British Empire, was the more popular of the two among the Irish in America.[147] The abortive raid which it organized against Canada in 1867 was, from an Irish point of view, absolutely mad, but it did reflect the hopes of many American expansionists in the years following the Civil War.[148] The Roberts faction, according to one of its critics, was more interested in annexing Canada to the United States than in winning Irish freedom.[149]

The Brotherhood, however, never conquered, and ran its course without an inch of soil over which to exercise sovereignty. It remained, as the *Freeman's Journal* liked to point out, "a mental Republic,"[150] existing precariously in the dangerous spiritual gulf that the Civil War had opened up between Great Britain and the United States. The abortive expedition of the O'Mahoney faction against the island of Campo Bello, then in dispute between the two countries, nicely illustrated how the Fenians exploited the tensions between Jonathan and John Bull.[151] But the Fenians were in turn exploited by the United States; both the administrations of Johnson and Grant used them as a threat to extort better terms from Great Britain in settling disputes arising out of the war.[152] And politicians of all parties and factions, in the scramble for power that developed during Reconstruction years, used the Fenians cynically and were so used by them.[153] Determined, as they said at the Chicago convention in 1863, to wipe out "the foul stigma which attaches to our name," and aware of the dangers to

[145] See *Freeman's Journal,* January 20, 1866.
[146] O'Leary, *Fenians and Fenianism,* II, 213; Letter of John Mitchel, Paris, to O'Mahoney, January 27, 1866. O'Donovan Rossa Papers, Catholic University of America Archives.
[147] D'Arcy, *op. cit.,* 106, 111, 140-141.
[148] D'Arcy, *op. cit.,* 171.
[149] Letter of F. F. Millen, Mexico, to John O'Mahoney, August 1, 1868. O'Donovan Rossa Papers, Catholic University of America Archives.
[150] December 23, 1865.
[151] D'Arcy, *op. cit.,* 135-140.
[152] D'Arcy, *op. cit.,* 129-132, 217-218, 325, 344.
[153] D'Arcy, *op. cit.,* 182 ff.

AMERICA AND THE IRISH PROBLEM, 1899-1921

Alan J. Ward

America and the Irish problem
1899–1921

The United States census of 1910 revealed that there were four and a half million people in the United States who had been born in Ireland, or who had at least one Irish-born parent. The figures did not reveal that many other Americans identified themselves with Ireland, the country of their grandparents, or even of their great-grandparents, and it was not unusual for Irish-American leaders at that time to claim the support of fifteen or twenty million fellow Irish-Americans. A great many of these had, indeed, managed to retain a sense of Irish identity and this was in part because they, or their forebears, had largely settled together in Irish ghettos in large cities. In addition they had been forced inwards to their Irish community for support when persecuted by the 'Know-nothings' and other nativist groups in the nineteenth century. This Irish sub-culture in which they lived was cultivated by three groups of fellow Irish-Americans who had an interest in promoting an Irish-American community, the better to control and command the Irish-Americans themselves; the Roman Catholic Church, which was very much an Irish Catholic Church in America, the Irish political bosses, interested in political power rather than Ireland, who had risen to power in the Democratic party by their ability to control the Irish vote, and a third group which utilized the audience they both nurtured, the Irish nationalists. The skill with which these nationalists mobilized Irish-Americans in support of Ireland's claim to independence added an important dimension to the British government's Irish problem for it became a problem for successive American governments too. As long as Ireland remained tied to England there were in America men and women prepared to emulate John Mitchel who had declared, when he first landed in New York in November 1853, that he intended to make use of the freedom guaranteed him in America to stimulate the movement for Irish independence.[1] It is the object of this paper

[1] *New York Tribune,* 20 Dec. 1853, cited in Florence Gibson, *The attitudes of the New York Irish towards state and national affairs, 1848–1891* (New York, 1951), p. 65.

64

to review, albeit briefly and incompletely, the significance of the activities of these Irish-American nationalists in the struggle for Irish freedom and in the development of Anglo-American relations during the period from the Boer war, which began in October 1899, to the Anglo-Irish treaty of December 1921.

The Boer war is a convenient starting point in that it marked the revival of Irish nationalism in both America and Britain after years of weakness and schism. In both countries the first major attack of the reunited Irish was on Britain's conduct of the war. In America it was the Irish who led in denouncing it, who organized mass meetings, provided huge audiences and the most popular orators. In Britain the breach in the Irish parliamentary party caused by the Parnell-O'Shea divorce scandal in 1890 was mended in the winter of 1899–1900, and in February 1900 John Redmond, the new Irish leader, spoke for Irishmen around the world when he declared in the house of commons:

It is true that whenever the empire is involved in a difficulty or complication which diminishes its great strength, a feeling of hope and satisfaction runs through the veins of the Irish race at home and abroad.[2]

The reunion in Ireland was not the result of any single factor, but one very important reason was the need to reestablish the supply of overseas aid, particularly American aid, to the political movement in Ireland. The Irish Land League had received hundreds of thousands of American dollars and the Irish party could not have paid living allowances to its members in parliament without overseas help. But these contributions largely disappeared in the 1890s because of the debilitating and very conspicuous divisions among the nationalists.[3] During an American fund raising mission in 1899 John Redmond was convinced that reunification at home was a precondition for Irish-American support in the future.[4] When he returned to America in the autumn of 1901 it was as the leader of a reunited Irish party and with the intention of establishing an American counterpart to the new United Irish League which had become the popular arm of the Irish party in Ireland. His major objective was money but tactically he wanted to establish in America a movement which would accept leadership and control from Ireland. He wanted the party in Ireland

[2] *Hansard 4 (commons)*, 7 Feb. 1900, lxxviii, cols 831–2.
[3] For an account of the financing of the Irish party see Lyons, *Ir. parl. party*, ch. 6.
[4] Tim Healy, *Letters and leaders of my day* (London, 1928), i, 443.

E

and at Westminster, rather than nationalists in America, to determine nationalist policy for Ireland. Redmond also wanted to keep the American movement out of the hands of those Irish-Americans who advocated the policy of revolutionary nationalism as the only route to national independence.[5] To do this he had to appear at least not to oppose such policies himself because the mass of Irish-Americans, whilst prepared to accept him as the leader of Ireland, were not inclined to appreciate the difference between revolutionary and constitutional nationalism or between the limited objective of home rule and complete national independence. To appeal to the maximum number of supporters in their overseas tours during the next ten or twelve years, therefore, Redmond and other members of the parliamentary party left a trail of ambiguous statements by which they appeared to endorse every position on Irish political autonomy, from moderate home rule to outright independence. The constitution of the United Irish League of America declared that its object was ' full national self-government for Ireland ' and although Redmond could be heard in the house of commons denying that he was a separatist, unionists certainly had evidence in plenty from America for their contention that home rule was but a first step to Irish independence and the dissolution of the British Empire.[6]

The United Irish League of America (U.I.L.) quickly became very powerful. Its numbers are not known but it was able to organize large meetings and great fund raising drives. It supplied the bulk of the money required for living-allowances which were paid to half of the Irish parliamentary party until salaries were introduced for all members of parliament in 1911. It also covered most of the expenses of one general election in 1906 and two in 1910. It was therefore important in bringing the parliamentary campaign for home rule to the very brink of victory by 1911.[7] The U.I.L. virtually monopolized Irish-American fund raising activities but when there were issues of international importance involving Great Britain and the U.S.A., the

[5] *New York Times,* 16 Nov., 5 Dec. 1901.

[6] For examples of these ambiguous declarations and the unionist attacks which resulted from them see Philip G. Cambray, *Irish affairs and the home rule question* (London, 1911); Ian Malcolm, M.P., ' Home rule all round ', in *Nineteenth Century,* Nov. 1910, lxviii, 791–9; *Hansard* 5 (*commons*), 15 Feb. 1911, xxi, cols 1076, 1105.

[7] The exact amount of money supplied from America is difficult to estimate, but from press reports, such records of the U.I.L. as are still available in America, and private papers, it appears that Lyons's estimate of £70,000 from foreign sources in the period 1900–10 is too low.

revolutionary faction of the Irish in America came to prominence in the leadership of the mass movement.

Revolutionary nationalists believed that Irish independence could only be achieved by the use of physical force. The Boer war reminded them that this was likely only if Britain was weakened by war. The revolutionary Irish movement in America had been terribly divided since the Fenian raids on Canada in the aftermath of the American civil war, but in 1900 the revolutionary Clan na Gael, founded in 1867, pulled itself together. It was directed by John Devoy, a New York journalist who on his arrival in the U.S.A. in 1871, fresh from imprisonment for Irish revolutionary activities, had immediately taken up the struggle again, and Daniel Cohalan, an American-born New York lawyer who was soon to become a justice of the supreme court of the state of New York. In their words, in 1900, ' our duty is to nerve and strengthen ourselves to wrest by the sword our political rights from England '.[8] This had always been Devoy's view. ' If Ireland wins her freedom ', he had written in 1881, ' she must wade to it through blood and suffering and sacrifice '.[9] The Clan kept the banner of revolution flying, both in America and Ireland. Together with United Irish societies, which were organized, usually by Clan members, in large American cities during the Boer war to coordinate the many other Irish-American organizations, it was in the vanguard of every attack on Britain. They drew upon much the same audiences as those supporting Redmond's United Irish League but Clan leaders themselves spent as much time attacking Redmond's Irish parliamentary party as they did fighting Britain. Their major vehicle was a new weekly newspaper, the *Gaelic American*, established by John Devoy in 1903 after Patrick Ford's well established and hitherto revolutionary *Irish World* had chosen to support Redmond. The *Irish World*, like the powerful Ancient Order of Hibernians in America, generally attacked Britain's policies throughout the world and advocated complete independence for Ireland, but accepted Redmond's constitutional gradualism as likely to be more effective than a revolution doomed to failure.

[8] Circular to Clan members, 10 Oct. 1900, cited in Charles C. Tansill, *America and the fight for Irish freedom, 1866–1922* (New York, 1957), p. 121. Tansill's book is an essential source but has to be used with caution. It is frequently incorrect and it is the opinion of this author that it presents a distorted view of the period being reviewed in this paper.
[9] Philip H. Bagenal, *The American Irish and their influence on Irish politics* (London, 1882), p. 223.

The Clan dreamed of a military rising in Ireland, although this possibility was receding as Ireland began to prosper through economic, agricultural and social reforms. The revolutionary Irish Republican Brotherhood had been weakened almost to the point of extinction by the Land League in the 1880s, by the agitation of the Irish parliamentary party under Parnell and now Redmond, and by this new sense of well-being. In 1907 Tom Clarke was sent from New York to reorganise the I.R.B., and henceforth Clan money and instructions were channelled through him.[10] The Clan supported Arthur Griffith's new Sinn Fein movement because it was separatist, but it exercised its most direct influence secretly through the I.R.B.

Despite this direct American intervention, the Irish revolutionary movement was seriously ill in the few years immediately preceding the first world war. The sickly indigenous Irish movement was dependent on the Clan na Gael which was itself dangerously weak. One of its leaders, John Keating, wrote despondently in 1910 that the end of the movement was near and that a dispute over the leadership had developed which emulated the disastrous schisms of the past. In 1913 Dr William Carroll expressed his great concern at the Clan's lack of funds and the success of the U.I.L.[11] But in the years since 1899 the Clan had helped to sustain the revolutionary movement in Ireland and had effectively influenced American policy towards Britain. Its objective had been to promote the view that American interests were incompatible with close Anglo-American relations. Irish-Americans did not force the American government to adopt new or particularly Irish policies, but they helped to set the limits within which the government was free to formulate its foreign policy. They influenced both public opinion and congress by leading and massively supporting attacks on Britain, by cultivating alliances with other groups hostile to Britain, by practising a bellicose brand of anglophobic Americanism, and by identifying themselves with traditional themes in American foreign policy, most notably non-alignment in the European balance of power and the inviolability of the western hemisphere—the Monroe doctrine. The mass audiences they organized were very often the same

[10] See Louis N. Le Roux, *Tom Clarke and the Irish freedom movement* (Dublin, 1936), pp 73 ff.

[11] The opposition from within the revolutionary movement was led by Mathew Cummings, militant national president of the Ancient Order of Hibernians, 1906–10. See Keating to Devoy 22 Jan. 1910, 11 Aug., 16 Nov. 1911 (N.L.I., MS 10,610, Devoy MSS); Carroll to Devoy, 7 Feb. 1913 (*Devoy's post-bag*, ii, 403–4).

as those mobilized by the United Irish League, for a great many Irish-Americans did not consider the incompatibility of the rival movements. They enjoyed public meetings as social occasions and relished every opportunity to bait the British. The *Irish World* could often be as vituperatively anglophobic as the *Gaelic American*, but as an organization the U.I.L. took little part in the anti-British campaign and the Clan and the United Irish societies led the way.

Britain and the United States were actually closer than ever before in 1900 and this disturbed the Clan. British neutrality during the Spanish-American war, America's own exercises in imperialism, the political power of an anglophile Republican élite, shared notions of an Anglo-Saxon culture, and a shared interest in obstructing the encroachments of continental European powers in China, all combined to bring Britain and America closer together. But Irish-Americans were determined to prevent closer cooperation between the two countries and, as John Redmond correctly observed at the American U.I.L. convention in 1904, 'if there is ever to be an Anglo-Saxon alliance it will be absolutely necessary to grant home rule to Ireland first'.[12] The members of the Clan na Gael opposed an alliance even on these terms, preferring to believe that England would always be an enemy to both Ireland and America, and they shared this antipathy with those Americans who distrusted Britain as the traditional enemy of the United States. Support for the Boers and a campaign attacking an alleged secret Anglo-American alliance were the major features of the Clan's attack on Britain during the early years of the century. Any enemy of Britain was, *ipso facto*, a friend to the Irish-Americans who joined with, and in very large part led, a pro-Boer coalition of anglophobes, German-Americans, who believed that an Anglo-American alliance could only be detrimental to Germany, and Democrat anti-imperialists. John Hay, the Republican secretary of state, confessed that it was as a result of these efforts, and in fear of congressional expressions of sympathy for the Boers, that President McKinley agreed to ask the British if they would accept American good offices in settling the war, an offer which Britain refused.[13] Hay himself was forced to declare publicly in 1900 that the United States had no secret alliance with Britain[14] and both major parties were forced to carry planks on

[12] *The Times,* 2 Sept. 1904.
[13] Allan Nevins, *Henry White: thirty years of American diplomacy* (New York, 1930), pp 151–2.
[14] John H. Ferguson, *American diplomacy and the Boer war* (Philadelphia, 1939), pp 122–3.

the Boer war in their election platforms later that year. The Democratic platform condemned the ' ill concealed Republican alliance with England ' to satisfy its Irish-American supporters.[15]

With the Republican party firmly in power for a variety of reasons, the pro-Boers in America could do little actually to help the Boers, though the United Irish societies of Chicago did send fifty or so volunteers to fight in South Africa in the disguise of a Red Cross contingent.[16] But it was quite clear that the agitation stirred by the Boer war was a serious stumbling block to the closer Anglo-American cooperation which many people on both sides of the Atlantic wanted. As an example, for a number of years the British government wanted to cooperate with the United States to promote their shared interest in preventing Russian and German expansion in the Far East, but, as John Hay explained in a letter to President Roosevelt in 1903, the combined opposition of Irish-Americans and German-Americans was sufficient to prevent Anglo-American cooperation in that area.[17]

Between 1897 and 1911 the United States negotiated four general arbitration treaties with Britain, and diplomats and statesmen on both sides of the Atlantic were agreed that the Irish were very important in the defeat of the three which were rejected by the senate, including the first in 1897 which cannot be discussed here. The treaty negotiated in 1904 was one of a number negotiated in identical terms with other countries, but the Irish were immediately involved in a campaign to denounce the treaty with Britain as an alliance. John Hay was still secretary of state when, in February 1905, he wrote to a friend that he had heard of no objections to the treaties until they were sent to the senate, where they were destroyed following attacks from two quarters, ' one from the Clan na Gael in New York and Philadelphia, who objected to nothing but the English treaty, and the other from certain interests in the south, who feared—utterly without cause—that the question of their repudiated debts might be brought into arbitration '.[18] The Clan would have loved this testimonial, for its leaders indeed believed that they had defeated the British treaty, but Hay overlooked, in this letter at least, the fact that senators had refused to ratify any of the treaties as they stood, and had amended them in

[15] Kirk H. Porter and Donald B. Johnson, *National party platforms, 1840-1960* (Urbana, Ill., 1961), pp 115, 124.
[16] *New York Times*, 26 Nov. 1900; Ferguson, op. cit., pp 66-67.
[17] Hay to Roosevelt, 28 Apr. 1903 (Library of Congress, John Hay MSS, box 26).
[18] Hay to Edwin D. Mead, 16 Feb. 1905 (ibid.).

a manner which completely eliminated their most important features, largely because they objected to the inroads which they believed the treaties made into their constitutional power in foreign relations. By agreeing to a general commitment for the U.S.A. to arbitrate future and unknown problems, the senate believed that it would lose the power to decide for itself the merits of each case as it arose. However, the senate's most dedicated supporters in the country at large were the Irish, and most of the mass meetings to oppose the treaties were organized by them. Both the British and American governments were prepared to testify to the effectiveness of their propaganda, and Hay's letter certainly illustrated his preoccupation with their influence.

In 1908 new arbitration treaties were accepted by the senate which were weak enough to conform to the senate's demands regarding its constitutional powers. Nevertheless the Irish led another campaign against the treaty with the British. The British ambassador, Lord Bryce, urged his government to consider the treaty quickly because Secretary of State Root was being bombarded with petitions by the Irish and was anxious that no delay in ratification should be attributed to their power.[19] Root himself wrote that the treaty was unanimously agreed by the senate foreign relations committee, ' notwithstanding an enormous number of petitions against the treaty from the Clan na Gael and other Irish societies '.[20]

In 1911 fresh arbitration treaties were negotiated which again appeared to the senate to attack its constitutional powers. The Irish, as always, saw the hand of perfidious Albion at work—of chaste America being seduced by an experienced roué—and it is amusing now to read this minute by Sir Eyre Crowe of the foreign office in March 1911 :

It would be interesting to see what the views of the Irish and German societies would be if they knew that the idea of the arbitration treaty originated with the U.S. and that it was rather embarrassing to H.M.G.[21]

These new treaties were defeated in March 1912 by the same device as in 1897 and 1904—crippling amendments were added in the senate which the administration would not accept or resubmit for renegotiation with the co-signatories. It was President Taft's intention, though

[19] Bryce to foreign sec., 10 Mar. 1908 (P.R.O., F.O. 371/563).
[20] Root to Ambassador Whitelaw Reid, 8 Apr. 1908 (Library of Congress, Elihu Root MSS, box 304).
[21] Minute by Crowe, 15 Mar. 1911, on Consul-General Bennett, New York, to foreign sec., 28 Feb. 1911 (P.R.O., F.O. 371/1270).

frustrated by his defeat in the November presidential election, to resubmit the treaties to the senate, but he believed that the Irish had been very influential in opposing them and that this attack had to be blunted. He believed that they might become more cooperative if he could secure the release of an Irish-American saboteur, Luke Dillon, who had been imprisoned in Canada for his part in an attempt to destroy the Welland Canal during the Boer war, and who had long been the subject of Clan appeals to the president. U.S. Ambassador Whitelaw Reid was given the task of approaching the Canadian prime minister, Borden, and the Canadian minister of justice, Doherty, both of whom were then in London for the coronation of George V. He failed to convince them at that time for the Canadians had their own Irish problem; they could do nothing for Dillon without antagonizing the large population of Orangemen in Ontario.[22] Dillon was not released until 1914, and then only on condition that the American-Irish would treat the whole matter quietly so that the protestant Canadian Irish would not be politically roused.[23]

Some other activities of the more militant Irish-Americans in the pre-World War I period can only be summarized here in a very few words. Their practice of cultivating allies has been mentioned already. At times they worked very closely with the opposition Democratic party and on occasions with members of both parties in the senate. They also cooperated with foreign powers and other immigrant communities in America. As Daniel Cohalan explained in a resolution which he presented to a Clan na Gael meeting in 1903, 'Ireland's true interests will . . . be best served by a steady, resolute, and progressive policy of organization among her own people the world over and the cultivation of alliances with England's enemies'.[24] The Irish, encouraged by both the *Gaelic American* and the *Irish World*, moved close to Russia and Russian diplomats in America, for example, with the signing of the Anglo-Japanese alliance in 1902, an agreement clearly directed against Russian expansion in the Far East.[25] Led by

[22] Taft to Reid, 7 July 1912; Reid to Taft, 24 July 1912 (Library of Congress, Whitelaw Reid MSS, boxes 91, 178).
[23] Keating to Devoy, 13 May 1914 (*Devoy's post-bag*, ii, 443–4).
[24] *New York Times*, 31 July 1903.
[25] Michael Davitt wrote articles for the *Irish World* from St Petersburg in February 1905. He argued, amongst other things, that the Russian government had nothing to fear from the labouring classes and that stories of massacres in Russia had been exaggerated by the British press. Jewish-Americans, many of them refugees from Russian persecution, were at that time actively protesting against Russian pogroms. The

the *Gaelic American*, the Clan also began a campaign in 1906 to publicise the Indian nationalist movement which caused the British great anxiety in America for about four years.[26]

It was in 1907 and 1908 that Irish-Americans showed signs of anticipating an Anglo-German war. They had cooperated with German-Americans before but had believed that Britain was more likely to go to war against France or Russia than against Germany. In January 1907, however, the American Ancient Order of Hibernians, then temporarily under very militant leadership, signed a formal agreement to cooperate with the German-American National Alliance, which indicated a new Irish interest in Germany,[27] and in July 1908 the Irish-American *Chicago Citizen* declared:

There is not an Irishman in America today, in whose veins good red blood is flowing, who would not rejoice to hear that a German army was marching in triumph across England from Yarmouth to Milford Haven.[28]

When the European war broke out in 1914 it became clear that this was a view shared by the great majority of the Irish in America. Redmond's pledges of Irish loyalty to the British Empire destroyed the once powerful United Irish League in America and cost him the support of the *Irish World*. By 1915 he was humbled into supporting the U.I.L. in America from Irish funds, a tragic reversal of the normal flow.[29] The Ancient Order of Hibernians, which had endorsed the parliamentary party at all but two of its biennial conferences since 1902, immediately declared its support for Germany. Militant anglo-phobes quickly took complete control of the Irish-American movement.

The pro-German Irish-Americans did not, however, inherit the sources of wealth of the U.I.L. In fact they were quite poor, and, for example, had been unable to provide more than a small part of the

Irish and the Jews were therefore pulling from opposite directions on the issue of Russo-American relations. See Alan J. Ward, ' Immigrant minority "diplomacy" : American Jews and Russia, 1901–1912 ', *Bulletin of the British Association for American Studies,* new series, no. 9, Dec. 1964, pp 8–9.

[26] British fears are well documented in the diplomatic records. See, for example, the correspondence of Bryce and Consul-General Bennett in P.R.O., F.O. 371/563, 783.

[27] John O'Dea, *The history of the Ancient Order of Hibernians and Ladies' Auxiliary* (Philadelphia, 1923), iii, 1387–8.

[28] *Chicago Citizen,* 11 July 1908, cited in Cambray, *Irish affairs and the home rule question,* pp 133–4.

[29] For the collapse of the U.I.L. in America see N.L.I., John Redmond MSS, P.C. 262 (1).

substantial sums in aid which the Irish Volunteers requested from them in 1914.[30] The Clan was able to organize and support Sir Roger Casement's mission to Germany with $10,000 but his requests for more money were rather embarrassing. Joseph McGarrity, a member of the Clan revolutionary directory, explained to him in July 1915 that only a small minority of Irish-Americans were active in the revolutionary movement, while the majority were indifferent; and that same month John Devoy wrote to McGarrity that the movement was going down, not up, and that the question of raising money was very serious.[31] Nevertheless the German Ambassador, Von Bernstorff, appreciated the importance of cooperating with the Irish. In September 1914 he recommended that his government should comply with Casement's wishes, that is, declare its support for the goal of Irish independence and allow Casement to organize an Irish brigade, drawn from captured British prisoners of war, which could be used to aid an Irish rebellion or in some other way to damage the British Empire. Bernstorff believed this would help the German case in the U.S.A. American public opinion, he reasoned, could best be influenced by promising independence to oppressed people, such as the Finns, the Poles, and the Irish.[32] The German government recognized his point. Casement was allowed to begin to recruit his Irish brigade, which proved to be an almost total failure, and in December the Germans signed an agreement that Ireland was entitled to her freedom when Britain was defeated.[33] However, U.S. Ambassador James Gerard, in Berlin, reported the rather bizarre news in January 1915 that the German under-secretary of state, Zimmerman, had told him that there were five hundred thousand trained German-Americans who would join the Irish and begin a revolution if the U.S.A. joined the Entente powers.[34] This was a grossly distorted image of the basic fact

[30] Only £1,000 were available to be sent to Clarke. See Devoy to Joseph McGarrity, 14, 18, 22 June 1914 (New York Public Library, Margaret McKim Maloney MSS, box 16).

[31] McGarrity to Casement, 10 July 1915 (Maloney MSS, boxes 1, 2); Devoy to McGarrity, 16 June 1915 (ibid., box 16).

[32] Von Bernstorff to German foreign ministry, 25 Sept. 1914 (*Documents relative to the Sinn Fein movement*, 1921), Cmd 1108, xxlx, 429, p. 3.

[33] René MacColl, *Roger Casement: a new judgement* (London, 1956), ch. VIII.

[34] Gerard to President Woodrow Wilson, 24 Jan., encl. in Wilson to Edward House, 28 Jan. 1915 (Library of Congress, R. S. Baker MSS, series 1, box 7).

that immigrant Americans did take sides in the war; for, as President Wilson wrote to U.S. Ambassador Page in London as early as October 1914, the several racial elements of the U.S.A. were daily becoming more restless and anxious to take sides. Everything possible had to be done, he wrote, to make it clear that the U.S.A. was neutral and prepared to defend neutral rights.[35]

Wilson's interpretation of neutrality was the traditional American one, that the U.S.A. should be free to sell to belligerents of both sides; and this, of course, helped the Entente, for Britain controlled the seas and therefore trade. Although, as McGarrity and Devoy testified, there were still very few Irish-Americans to support a revolutionary conspiracy against Britain, huge numbers of them joined German-Americans in attacking this traditional view by calling for a complete embargo on trade with belligerents, as they had done for similar reasons during the Boer war. They also resisted any suggestion that America should intervene on the side of the Entente. Their German-American and Irish-American leaders joined forces in various organizations—the American Embargo Conference, the Friends of Peace, the American Neutrality League, the American Truth Society, and others—and packed mass protest meetings throughout the country. The British government became very worried and considered starting an active counter propaganda in America, particularly one demonstrating Ireland's loyalty to the British Empire to be conducted by touring Irish politicians,[36] but the advice of Britain's ambassador, Spring Rice, was that this would exacerbate the problem of American opinion.[37] Secretary of State William Jennings Bryan hastened to assure the British early in 1915 that although the Irish- and German-Americans were pro-German in their sympathies they would not be allowed to determine American policy on trade with belligerents.[38] Nevertheless the British did inject articles, pamphlets, and books on the Irish war-effort, written by John Redmond and others, into the

---

[35] Wilson to Page, 26 Oct. 1914 (Library of Congress, Woodrow Wilson MSS, series VII, letter book 17a, pp 479–82).

[36] Sir Edward Grey to Ambassador Cecil Spring Rice, 13 Aug. 1915 (Yale University Library, Edward House MSS, drawer 9, file 8).

[37] Spring Rice to Grey, 19 Aug. 1915 (*Letters and friendships of Sir Cecil Spring Rice,* ed. Stephen Gwynn, London, 1929), ii, 278–9.

[38] Arthur S. Link, *Wilson: the struggle for neutrality, 1914–1916* (Princeton, 1960), p. 185.

regular, rather quiet, American propaganda campaign already being conducted by Gilbert Parker from London.[39]

The German government cooperated directly with the Irish- and German-Americans and financed some of their joint activities. Liaison with Irish-Americans was handled by the German military attaché, Franz von Papen, and two German agents, Wolf von Igel and George von Skal, in New York.[40] Fortunately for the British, the espionage and sabotage activities of the German and Austro-Hungarian governments were being widely attacked in the press by late 1915, as a result of their own mistakes,[41] and the U.S. government also began a campaign against the activities of hyphenated Americans, notably Irish- and German-Americans, for their attempts to influence American neutrality policy.[42] This had an effect on public opinion but it was still clear that U.S. foreign policy was being circumscribed by the necessity to balance the ethnic scales in America. In 1916 Robert Lansing, the new secretary of state, prayed that the United States would not be drawn into the war prematurely. The United States differed from other countries, he wrote in his diary, for its people were not united by ties of blood. The United States still lacked nationality ' in its ethnological sense '.[43]

1916 was, of course, the year of the Easter rising, in which Irish-Americans played an important role, and its consequences seriously damaged Anglo-American relations. Liaison between Ireland and Germany on the rising was managed by the Clan na Gael in America, which also managed to supply financial help, but this proved to be a cumbersome avenue for the Irish. German arms for the rebellion which were sent on the ill-fated ship, the *Aud*, went astray when revised instructions for a rendezvous and for landing them arrived in Berlin too late, after travelling by sea to New York and then back to Europe by coded cable. The *Aud*, fully loaded, but travelling

---

[39] James D. Squires, *British propaganda at home and in the United States, 1914–1917* (Cambridge, Mass., 1935), appendix. See also John Redmond, *The Irish nation and the war* (Dublin, 1915), and S. Parnell Kerr, *What the Irish regiments have done* (London, 1916).

[40] John Devoy, *Recollections of an Irish rebel* (New York, 1929), ch. LIV.

[41] Link, *Wilson: neutrality*, pp 554–56, 561–4, 645–50; Link, *Wilson: confusion and crisis, 1915–1916* (Princeton, 1964), pp 56–9.

[42] See ibid., pp 34–7, for Wilson's address to congress, 7 Dec. 1915.

[43] Lansing diary, 9 Jan. 1916 (Library of Congress, Robert Lansing MSS, box 2, i, 37).

without a radio, was scuttled by her crew after being seized by a British patrol off the Irish coast.[44]

It has been suggested that the American government betrayed the rebellion because on 18 April American authorities raided the New York office of the German agent, Wolf von Igel, and discovered details of German and Irish-American collusion in the rising which was timed to begin within a few days. The State Department did pass this information to the British embassy, but not promptly enough, and it arrived in England too late to affect the beginning of the rising or the capture of Casement.[45] In any case Casement's last minute submarine trip was not mentioned in the captured documents. Despite some prior warning by their own intelligence services, the British were in almost total disarray when the rising began. General Friend, the commander-in-chief, Ireland, was on leave in England and the bulk of the British officers stationed in Dublin were at the races when the rising began.[46] However, the Von Igel papers were very useful to the American government as a bargaining counter in critical negotiations then under way concerning German submarine attacks on American and other neutral shipping, the most notorious case having been the sinking of the *Lusitania*. Part of a bargain struck in May 1916, which involved a German retreat on this whole issue, was an American agreement that the Von Igel papers would not be published.[47] The American public would have demanded a more drastic settlement of the submarine question had it known of German conspiracies to sabotage American industry, and to foment rebellions in Ireland and India, which the Von Igel papers revealed. Details were actually not released to the press until September 1917, when they were used in

[44] See Devoy, *Recollections,* pp 458–63; *Documents relating to the Sinn Fein movement,* pp 9–12, and Karl Spindler, *The mystery of the Casement ship* (Berlin, 1931), passim.

[45] Secret memo. on Ireland, 2 May 1916 (Bodl., Asquith MSS, box 42). See also Spring Rice to Sir Horace Plunkett, 4 May 1916, in which he confesses how little he knew of the plans for the rising (London, Plunkett Foundation for Cooperative Studies, Plunkett MSS). The Von Igel papers are in Washington D.C., National Archives, State Dept. records 701.6211.

[46] See R. H. Brede, for army council, to C. in C. home forces, 28 Apr. and copy of reply May 1916, also secret memo on Ireland, 2 May 1916 (Asquith MSS, box 42).

[47] See House to Wilson, 14 May 1916 (Wilson MSS, series II, box 97), and Lansing to Attorney General Thomas W. Gregory, 21 Sept. 1916 (Lansing MSS, v, 21).

a calculated campaign to silence Irish-Americans after the United States had entered the war on the side of the Entente.[48]

Britain's brutal suppression of the rising, though understandable in the context of the war, marked a turning point for the militant Irish movements in Ireland and America. The proclamation of independence had called for the support of Ireland's 'exiled children in America', and they responded as the British executed and imprisoned Irishmen in the immediate aftermath of the rising. After the first rush of executions the British realized that the impact on American opinion was disastrous. Lloyd George is reputed to have said that Irish-American opinion could swing America towards Germany and that the U.S.A. might break the British blockade on the central powers. Something had to be done to satisfy America. In the cabinet both Arthur Balfour and Sir Edward Grey supported this view.[49] Lloyd George agreed to try to find a settlement to the Irish problem and failed, but Americans took no notice of his attempt because it coincided with the Casement trial and appeal in June and July 1916.[50]

The British cabinet insisted on Casement's execution because of his treason in Germany; because, despite evidence to the contrary which they already had, they persisted in believing that he was a leader and probably the guiding spirit of the rebellion,[51] and because a great many people in Britain demanded that he be hanged. At least a dozen times between April and July, Spring Rice warned them against the execution because it could lead only to Casement's martyrdom in America.[52] The American press, whilst generally accepting his guilt, questioned the wisdom of his execution, and the United States senate, though rejecting resolutions which mentioned Casement by name, accepted one in July which appealed to Britain to exercise clemency

[48] Released by the Committee on Public Information for publication in newspapers dated Sunday, 23 Sept., 1917.

[49] Michael MacDonagh, *The life of William O'Brien* (London, 1928), p. 225; cabinet memo. by Asquith for the king, 27 June 1916 (P.R.O., CAB. 41/37 (24)).

[50] Denis Gwynn, *The history of partition, 1912–1925* (Dublin, 1950), pp. 147–56.

[51] General Maxwell to Lord French, 13 May 1916 (Asquith MSS, box 44); Maxwell to Asquith, 28 May, 1916 (ibid., box 37). The cabinet had seen the report on Casement's interrogation from which it would have been very difficult sensibly to conclude that he was the leader. See printed cabinet document May 1916 sent to Spring Rice by Eric Drummond, 3 May 1916 (F.O. 115/2073) and H. Montgomery Hyde (ed.), *The trial of Roger Casement* (London, 1960), pp xxxiii–xxxvi.

[52] F.O. 115/2073.

in the treatmeint of all Irish political prisoners.[53] There were at least five discussions of the Casement execution and its effect on American opinion in the British cabinet in July and August,[54] and to try to counter American sympathy the government authorized a campaign to attack Casement's character by showing copies of the now notorious ' black diaries ' to American and British journalists in Britain and America.   Spring Rice requested copies to show to influential Americans, and details were communicated to Ambassador Page who advised the president against aiding Casement in any way.[55]   This campaign was relatively ineffective, but Casement was nevertheless executed on 3 August. President Wilson himself had refused to inter- vene for strictly legal and diplomatic reasons and not because of the diaries. He insisted throughout that the U.S.A. had absolutely no grounds for intervening in the British legal process on behalf of a British citizen.[56]

The brutal suppression of the Easter rising certainly damaged British prestige in America. On 16 May, 1916, for example, Wilson write to Colonel House that the at least temporary removal of the German submarine crisis concentrated American attention on Britain's intolerable interference with American trade to and from neutral countries in Europe, and he added that Americans had been shocked by the suppression of the rising.[57] Ambassador Von Bernstorff was able to report to his government in August that American feelings towards Germany were noticeably more friendly because of Britain's interference with American trade and the execution of Casement.[58]

[53] U.S., *Congressional Record*, 64 congress, 1 session, 1916, v. 53, pt. 11, pp 11429 ff., and pt. 12, pp 11773 ff.

[54] CAB. 41/37 (25, 26, 27, 28, 29).

[55] MacColl, *Roger Casement*, pp 289–90; Hyde, op. cit., p. lxv. The British naval attaché, Capt. Guy Gaunt, was responsible for disseminating copies of the diary in New York. See James J. Walsh to W. J. M. A. Maloney, 3 Aug. 1938 (Maloney MSS, box 20); John Quinn to Patrick McCartan, 31 Jan. 1919 (ibid., box 21); Spring Rice to Quinn, 26 Aug. 1916 (ibid., boxes 19–20). Spring Rice made his request to Grey on 19 and 20 July 1916 (F.O. 115/2073).

[56] For example, Wilson to Tumulty, 2 May 1916, and Wilson's note to Tumulty, 20 July 1916, on M. F. Doyle to Tumulty, 6 July 1916 (Wilson MSS, series VI, box 520, file 3085).

[57] Arthur S. Link, *Wilson: campaigns for progressivism and peace, 1916–1917* (Princeton, 1965), pp 20–21.

[58] Von Bernstorff to German foreign ministry, 8 Aug. 1916, inter- cepted by the British and enclosed in Page to Wilson, 3 Dec. 1917 (Wilson MSS, series II, box 131).

In April 1917 the United States joined the war on the side of the Allies for reasons which the Irish- and German-American agitations could do nothing to influence. Irish-American revolutionary activities immediately dwindled and the *Gaelic American* suffered a loss of support which nearly ended its career. The Irish-American leaders now adopted two policies. The first was to act circumspectly, to convince other Americans that the Irish were loyal, and with minor exceptions they succeeded. Secondly, they worked to have Irish independence included in the peace settlement. The president had already helped by insisting that World War I was a war for the freedom of small nations, and he had widely publicized the principle of national self-determination which could clearly be applied to Ireland, although this was not his intention. Wilson had little sympathy with the organized Irish in America. He believed that their leaders had been disloyal during the period of neutrality and he nursed a special hatred of Judge Cohalan, but he was not hostile to Ireland as such. He told Irish-Americans who were known to be friendly to his administration that he was doing what he could for Ireland,[59] and in fact, just four days after the United States declared war, he instructed Ambassador Page in London to explain to the British government that the only circumstance standing in the way of an absolutely cordial cooperation with Britain by all Americans who were not tied to Germany by their immigrant origins was Britain's failure to resolve the problem of Irish self-government. Americans would respond enthusiastically, he promised, if a solution could be found.[60] Page took up the question with Lloyd George, now prime minister, and members of the cabinet who dined with him on 17 April. Lloyd George told him that he was aware of the American problem and was trying to solve the Irish problem. 'God knows I'm trying', he said, 'tell the president that'. But he added, when pointing to Sir Edward Carson across the room, 'madmen, madmen—I never saw any such task'. He told Page that the president should discuss the problem with Arthur Balfour, the British foreign secretary, who went to Washington late in April.[61] Balfour was indeed instructed by the cabinet to study

---

[59] Joseph Tumulty to John D. Crimmins with a note attached by Wilson, 5 May, 1917 (Library of Congress, Joseph Tumulty MSS, box 2).

[60] Wilson to Lansing, 10 Apr. 1917 (R. S. Baker MSS, series 1, box 11).

[61] Page to Wilson, 4 May 1917 (Wilson MSS, series II, box 118). See also Page to Lansing ('Confidential for the president'), 18 Apr. 1917 (State Dept., 841d.00/106).

the influence of the Irish question in America, and he reported to the prime minister in May that it was ' apparently the only difficulty we have to face here, and its settlement would no doubt greatly facilitate the vigorous and lasting cooperation of the United States government in the war '.[62]

Later in May, Lloyd George announced the creation of the Irish convention, certainly partly in response to the American agitation, although the cabinet did discuss it as early as March before the U.S.A. entered the war.[63] The convention first sat in July 1917 and continued well into 1918, conveniently freezing the Irish problem for that period. Furthermore, it enable Lloyd George and his colleagues to say, as they did several times in later years, that they had offered Ireland self-determination in the convention but that the Irish had failed to agree among themselves.[64] The *Irish World* and the *Gaelic American*, however, immediately saw it as a device to trap Ireland into appearing to be responsible for England's failure to keep her word.

The collapse of the convention was predetermined by the conflicts within Ireland itself, but it coincided with the Irish conscription crisis of 1918, when Lloyd George again testified to the importance of the Irish question in American policy. In April 1918 he announced that conscription was to be extended to Ireland, a move which revolutionaries had prayed for since 1914, believing that it would set off a rebellion in Ireland.[65] Lloyd George knew that it would cause trouble. ' What would be the result? ', he had already asked his friend Lord Riddell in February 1917; ' scenes in the house of commons, a possible rupture with America, which is hanging in the balance, and serious disaffection in Canada, Australia and South Africa '. To support at least part of his contention, we should note that Prime Minister Billy Hughes of Australia had already made it quite clear to the cabinet that Irish-Australian opposition had caused the defeat of his conscription proposals in the Australian referendum of 1916, a result which was to be repeated in 1917.[66] Lloyd George continued to Riddell:

[62] Balfour to Lord Robert Cecil, 5 May 1917 (F.O. 115/2244).
[63] War cabinet meeting 101 (1, 2), 22 Mar. 1917, and other meetings in CAB. 23/2.
[64] Bonar Law in debate 29 July 1918, *Hansard 5 (commons)*, cix, cols 85 ff; Chief Sec. Shortt in debate, 5 Nov. 1918, ibid., cx, cols 1962 ff; Lloyd George in debate 21 July 1919, ibid., cxviii, vols 995 ff.
[65] The O'Rahilly to Devoy, 10 Nov. 1914 (Devoy, *Recollections*, pp 414-15); McGarrity to Casement, 9 Nov. 1915 (Maloney MSS, box 1).
[66] War cabinet meeting 24 (11), 1 Jan. 1917 (CAB. 23/1).

F

They would say, ' You are fighting for the freedom of nationalities. What right have you to take this little nation by the ears and drag it into war against its will? ' If you passed the act you would only get 160,000 men. You could only get them at the point of a bayonet.[67]

These problems still existed in April 1918 when the government, desperate for men, under pressure from the military and the unionists, and convinced that the exemption of Ireland would mean a breach of faith with those already, or about to be, conscripted elsewhere, decided on conscription in the full knowledge that it might produce civil war. The advice from Ireland, from the lord lieutenant, the chief secretary, the head of the Royal Irish Constabulary and unionist leaders, as well as from nationalists of all kinds, was that conscription would lead to chaos and disaster.[68]

From America Lord Reading, the new British ambassador, warned that the effect there would be bad.[69] Wilson's secretary, Joseph Tumulty, had already urged on him the importance to America of immediate Irish home rule.[70] The cabinet agreed that Balfour should put the British case for conscription to the Americans. He therefore sent to Colonel House on 2 April a long cable which listed the necessity for Irish conscription and the problems associated with it, including the political and military dangers. He concluded by asking what the effect of Irish conscription would be in America. House replied that it would accentuate the Irish problem in America.[71] The government next cabled Sir William Wiseman, Britain's confidential liaison official with House and the president in America, for his views. Wiseman replied on 5 April, quite misleadingly, that America would accept conscription if the government did something for Ireland immediately on the lines of Redmond's moderate home rule demands.[72] When Lloyd George presented the conscription proposals to parliament it was with this advice in mind and not the warnings of Reading and House. He made it quite clear that Wilson's conduct of the war was

[67] George Allardice Riddell, Baron Riddell, *Lord Riddell's war diary, 1914–1918* (London, 1933), p. 239.
[68] War cabinet meetings 374 (12) and 375 (2), 27 Mar. 1918 (CAB. 23/5).
[69] Ibid., 379A (2), 1 Apr. 1918 (CAB. 23/14).
[70] Tumulty and Reading used Shane Leslie as intermediary. See Leslie to Tumulty, 23 Apr. 1918 (Wilson MSS, series vi, box 520, file 3926).
[71] Balfour to House, 2 Apr. 1918 (Yale University Library, Sir William Wiseman MSS, drawer 90, file 69) and House to Balfour, 3 Apr. 1918 (ibid., file 64).
[72] Eric Drummond to Wiseman and reply, 5 Apr. 1918 (ibid., file 69).

being hampered by Britain's failure to solve the Irish problem. ' American opinion ', he said, ' supports the justice of the man-power [conscription] bill, provided self-government is offered to Ireland '. He knew that much labour and liberal opinion in parliament agreed with this condition, and he therefore promised that Ireland would be granted a measure of self-government, though he made no attempt to define its terms.[73] In fact, of course, opposition in Ireland to conscription was too strong, even after parliamentary approval, for it to be implemented, and no measure of home rule the government could devise was acceptable equally to Sinn Fein, the nationalists, and Ulster. Lloyd George expressed his disappointment in the house of commons. ' Not to settle [the Irish problem] ', he said, ' is not merely increasing our difficulties in conducting the war, it is increasing the difficulties of the United States of America in conducting the war '.[74] Fortunately the war ended within a few months.

On both sides of the Atlantic the Irish, supported by the massive Sinn Fein victory in the general election of December 1918, immediately appealed to the principle of ' national self-determination ' which was to be a major feature of the peace settlement. Eamon de Valera, Arthur Griffith and Count Plunkett were delegated by Dail Eireann to present the Irish rebublic's case for recognition to the peace conference,[75] and although they were not allowed to go to Paris three prominent Irish-Americans did go. They were appointed by a massive Irish Race Convention held in Philadelphia in February 1919, which had been arranged by the Friends of Irish Freedom, an organization founded by the leaders of the Clan na Gael in March 1916 and now totally dominating Irish-American activities.[76] The three delegates

[73] *Hansard 5 (commons)*, 16 Apr. 1918, cv, cols 343 ff.
[74] Ibid., 25 June, 1918, v, 107, cols 957 ff.
[75] Macardle, *Ir. republic* (London, 1937), pp 283–9.
[76] Tansill, *America and the fight for Irish freedom*, pp 296–302. The three delegates were Frank P. Walsh, former chairman of the Commission on Industrial Relations and joint president of the National War Labor Board, Edward F. Dunne, a former mayor of Chicago and former governor of Illinois, both of whom were well known to the president, plus Michael J. Ryan, a Philadelphia lawyer and formerly national president of the United Irish League in America. Frank Walsh described the activities of the delegates to the senate committee on foreign relations. See U.S., Congress, Senate, Committee on Foreign Relations, *Treaty of peace with Germany: hearings before the committee on foreign relations,* 66 congress, 1 session, 1919, Senate doc. 106, pt. 17, pp 799 ff. House recorded his impressions of their dealings with him in his diary, vols 15 and 16 (House MSS).

first attempted to force the American peace commissioners officially to ask the British for safe-conduct passes for De Valera and his party but they failed. Then they were refused permission to put Ireland's claims to the peace conference themselves. President Wilson apologetically admitted to them that when he first announced his support for the principle of self-determination he had no idea of the hopes he would stimulate in so many aspiring nations, some of which he had never heard of, but the peace conference, with his support, quite predictably refused to consider any case for self-determination which did not relate to the disposition of territory formerly held by the defeated central powers.

Colonel House unofficially, but with Wilson's approval, did put the three Irish-American delegates in touch with British officials and Lloyd George allowed them to visit Ireland to inspect conditions for themselves, because he mistakenly thought that Wilson wanted them to do this. The effect in Ireland, however, was considerable, for the delegates made it quite clear that they supported 'President' de Valera and the Irish Republic. They were given a fine reception and the new chief secretary for Ireland, MacPherson, told the cabinet that he believed the rebellion grew worse in Ireland following their, as it were, 'encouraging' visit.[77]

There was intense American interest in Ireland's case during the peace conference. Over Wilson's objections the house of representatives agreed on 4 March, 1919, by a vote of 216 to 45, that the peace conference should favourably consider Ireland's claim to self-determination.[78] Wilson dreaded the effect of this resolution on British public opinion, which he had to consider in Paris. It was not a question of sympathy, he told Tumulty, but of tactics, at a very critical time.[79] By this he meant that he needed British support for his private ambition, the establishment of a League of Nations, and he could do nothing publicly for Ireland without jeopardizing its success. He was further embarrassed when, on 6 June, the U.S. senate, by a massive margin of 60 to 1, resolved that De Valera, Griffith and Plunkett should be allowed to appear before the peace conference and simultaneously expressed its sympathy with the Irish claim to self-determination.[80]

[77] War cabinet meeting 567A, 14 May 1919 (CAB. 23/15).
[78] U.S., *Congressional record*, 65 congress, 3 session, 1919, v. 57, pp 3174, 5027–57.
[79] Wilson to Tumulty, 7, 30 Jan. 1919 (Tumulty MSS, box 2).
[80] U.S., *Congressional record*, 66 congress, 1 session, 1919, v. 58, pt. 1, pp 728 ff.

Joseph Tumulty repeatedly asked Wilson to say something to demonstrate his sympathy for Ireland and during the President's brief return to America in February and March, Tumulty did pressure him, very much against his will, into meeting a deputation from the Philadelphia Irish Race Convention. Tumulty believed that the Irish question was crucial to the state of American opinion and could very seriously affect the fate of the peace treaty in America.[81] He was proved correct when Irish-Americans played a vital role in the defeat of the treaty and the covenant of the League of Nations which it contained. A vast campaign against the league was launched by the Friends of Irish Freedom, led by Daniel Cohalan. It was financed by an Irish 'victory fund' which had been opened at the Irish Race Convention in Philadelphia in February. This campaign taught once again, what Redmond knew, that the interests of the Irish leaders overseas could not necessarily be equated with the interests of Ireland. In this case the funds and energies of the Irish in America were directed more to destroying 'Britain's league' than to helping Ireland.

The leaders of the Friends established close alliances with Henry Cabot Lodge, chairman of the senate foreign relations committee and leader of the senate 'reservationists', and with William Borah, leader of the senate's Republican 'irreconcilables' who were opposed to any League of Nations. The Irish became the leading weapon of the anti-league forces outside congress and they contributed substantially to the failure of the peace treaty. It was they who organized the largest meetings and took full-page advertisements in newspapers along the route of Wilson's speaking-tour in September. In hearings before the senate committee on foreign relations and in the campaign in the country at large, the Irish insisted that the United States should not sign a treaty which guaranteed Britain's ill-gotten empire and contained no provision which could guarantee independence to Ireland.[82] Their arguments were frequently inaccurate and often bizarre, but the scale and volume of their attack was impressive and the senate even agreed to add a reservation to the peace treaty supporting Ireland's aspirations for self-government.[83] The senate had

[81] See, for example, Tumulty to Wilson, 29, 31 Dec. 1918, 28 Jan. 1919 (Tumulty MSS, box 2); 5, 28 Feb., 1 Mar., 9 June 1919; Tumulty to Admiral Grayson, 7 June 1919 (ibid. box 3).

[82] See, for example, Library of Congress, William Borah MSS, boxes 550–51, and *Hearings re. peace treaty*, pp 757 ff.

[83] Denna F. Fleming, *The United States and the League of Nations* (New York, 1932), ch. XVII.

primarily attacked the League of Nations because many senators believed that it eroded the senate's constitutional powers in foreign relations and challenged traditional American foreign policies. This constitutional argument had also been the senators' major objection to the arbitration treaties of 1897, 1904, and 1911, when Irish-Americans had again been their best allies.

Eamon de Valera secretly arrived in New York in June 1919, and was in the U.S.A. for much of the campaign against the peace treaty. He remained there for eighteen months as 'president of the Irish republic' without a protest from the British or American governments. Neither of them was prepared to antagonize American opinion in view of the fine, and often rapturous, reception he received. By the time they finally discussed the problem of his use of America to stimulate the rebellion in Ireland, in December 1920, he was already on his way back to Ireland, in secret as he had arrived.[84]

In America De Valera insisted that the American Irish should subordinate themselves to his direction as the chosen leader of Ireland. He received a series of rebuffs from the executive of the Friends of Irish Freedom and found himself engaged in a personal battle for control with Daniel Cohalan, who dominated the Friends. Cohalan particularly disputed De Valera's self-asserted right to direct Irish-Americans on the ground that the Irish-American movement was indeed American and had to be managed in a way which would be consistent with American interests. Cohalan believed that an American war with Britain over the issue of commercial superiority was inevitable and he saw any League of Nations as both un-American and as a British plot to enslave the United States in the interests of the British Empire. De Valera had no objection to a League of Nations provided that Ireland was a member; he had no real objection to British control of the seas, again if Ireland was free, and there is no reason to believe that he anticipated or welcomed the thought of an Anglo-American war. He had no reason to hate Wilson, or to prefer the company of Republicans, and he counted a number of Democratic senators and congressmen among his supporters.[85]

[84] Memo. of conversation between Under-Secretary of State Norman Davis and Ambassador Geddes, 19 Dec. 1920 (Library of Congress, Norman Davis MSS, box 9).

[85] The dispute between De Valera and Cohalan is discussed in a number of books with differing interpretations. For example, Macardle, *Ir. republic*, Tansill, *America and the fight for Irish freedom*, Patrick McCartan, *With de Valera in America* (Dublin, 1932), Denis R. Gwynn,

De Valera was dissatisfied with those directing the Irish-Americans and at the amount of financial aid Ireland was receiving from America. Up to the end of 1920 the Irish ' victory fund ' had contributed only $115,000 to the nationalist movement in Ireland, but had spent about $750,000 in the United States, mostly in its campaign against the league.[86] De Valera therefore set about destroying the power of Cohalan and the Friends of Irish Freedom. In January 1920, with the cooperation of the Friends, who could hardly refuse to help the ' president', notwithstanding the fact that they were destroying themselves, De Valera was able to inaugurate an Irish bond-certificate drive. Irish bond-certificates were sold with the promise that they could be exchanged for Irish Republican bonds soon after international recognition of an Irish republic.[87] Five and a half million dollars were subscribed, far outstripping even the large amounts raised in previous American campaigns, and four million dollars were actually spent in Ireland (only $400,000 ultimately ended up in the treasury of the Irish Free State). The Irish ' victory fund ' was closed.[88]

Next, in November 1920, De Valera was able to establish an American Association for the Recognition of the Irish Republic, which soon eclipsed the Friends as the popular Irish movement in America.[89] The Friends continued to pour our great masses of anti-British propaganda but their membership was drastically cut. De Valera now controlled a popular movement in America and a huge source of funds. Furthermore, the American Commission on Conditions in

De Valera (London, 1933), Mary C. Bromage, *De Valera and the march of a nation* (New York, 1956), Katherine O'Doherty, *Assignment America: de Valera's mission to the United States* (New York, 1957). Cohalan's belief in an Anglo-American war was described by him in, amongst others, *Freedom of the seas*, published by the Friends of Irish Freedom in 1919, and ' America's advice to Ireland', in William G. Fitz-Gerald (ed.), *The voice of Ireland* (London, 1924).

[86] Tansill, op. cit., p. 347.

[87] Ibid., pp 347–53.

[88] The amount of money remaining in the U.S.A. was later the subject of extended litigation between the Irish Free State and republicans in Irish and American courts. Over two and a half million dollars were finally distributed to certificate holders in 1930. See Macardle, *Ir. republic,* pp 1024–5; O'Doherty, op. cit., pp 66–9; State Dept. 841d. 51/--; Maloney MSS, boxes 19, 22.

[89] Estimates of the size of the A.A.R.I.R. are unreliable. The figure of 800,000 members in Macardle, *Ir. republic,* p. 426, is probably too high but Tansill, op. cit., p. 395n illustrates the decline in membership of the F.O.I.F. to only 20,000 from almost 101,000 regular members.

Ireland which, in 1921, widely publicized a rather distorted view of the suffering inflicted by the war in Ireland, and the American Committee for Relief in Ireland which, beginning in 1921, supplied about $5 million for Irish relief, were controlled by Americans who were supporters of De Valera. These activities also attracted the attention and support of many Americans who were not of Irish extraction.[90] By 1921, then, Ireland was again being massively supported by the American Irish as in the pre-war period. The mass movement in America generally looked, once again, to Ireland for leadership, and De Valera had taken up where John Redmond left off in 1914, despite his commitment to very different principles.

De Valera had completely failed to secure American recognition for the Irish Republic and had shown his political inexperience with some clumsy moves in America,[91] but he had sponsored a new and more constructive American interest in Ireland which overshadowed the narrow anglophobia of the Clan na Gael and the Friends of Irish Freedom. Without Cohalan's dominating genius, the Irish-Americans could not again be the force they had only recently been in American politics. Furthermore, the victory of their allies, the Republicans, in the 1920 elections, did nothing to enhance the power of the Friends—rather the reverse. The alliance had been forged in opposition to the Democratic administration and the League of Nations covenant, and now that both had been defeated the association had no value to the party in power. Irish-Americans still embarrassed the British, but the burden of this embarrassment was felt in Britain's relations with Ireland, now being massively supported by Americans, rather than in her relations with America. An exception occurred in May 1921 when Secretary of State Hughes, by warning that their refusal would rebound seriously on American opinion and hence on Anglo-American relations, forced the British to allow money raised by the American Committee for Relief in Ireland to be distributed in

---

[90] See *Report of the American Committee for Relief in Ireland,* published by the committee in 1922; *Evidence on the conditions in Ireland,* and *Interim report* published by the American Commission on Conditions in Ireland, 1921. W. J. M. A. Maloney was the guiding spirit of both movements.

[91] For example, his letter attacking Cohalan and the *Gaelic American,* in Gwynn, *De Valera,* pp 96–101; his appearance at the Republican Party national convention, ibid., pp 106–7, Tansill, op. cit., pp 373–83, MacCartan, op. cit., pp 198–9; his interview published by the *Westminster Gazette* on 6 Feb. 1920.

Ireland although Britain knew it would be used for republican purposes and was largely unnecessary for relief.[92]

It was clear that Americans could continue to aid the Irish in their struggle almost indefinitely. It was also quite clear from conversations that the U.S. consul in Dublin, Dumont, had with Arthur Griffith that Sinn Fein believed the Irish were a decisive force in American politics and that America would soon have to support Ireland's claims.[93] In Dumont's view, 'the movement is kept very much alive by reports of the great progress the cause of Irish freedom is making in the United States'.[94] Nevertheless there is some evidence that the funds from America, though larger than ever before, were insufficient to sustain the high level of the war in Ireland, and that shortage of money was one reason for the truce in July 1921.[95] In the meantime Britain had already made a very important concession to American opinion, which facilitated the final settlement later that year. In December 1919 a British cabinet committee on the Irish question reported to the full cabinet that, in view of the situation in Ireland itself, of public opinion in Great Britain, and still more of public opinion in the dominions and the United States of America, it was not possible to repeal or postpone the home rule act. The peace conference had dealt with so many analogous questions in Europe, the report continued, that the British government had to make a sincere attempt to settle the Irish question. The committee agreed that there should be partition, for Ulster could not be forced into a Dublin parliament against its will, but in order to satisfy opinion in the United States and the dominions it proposed that two parliaments should be established in Ireland. It could thus be made to appear that the government was offering home rule to the whole of Ireland, or rather self-determination to both Irelands.[96] Arthur Balfour was one who argued in the cabinet that, if offered self-determination, Ulster

[92] The money was handled in Ireland by the Sinn Fein controlled Irish White Cross. See cabinet paper no. 2921, 9 May 1921 (CAB. 24/123); cabinet meeting 36/21 (4), 10 May 1921 (CAB. 23/25); memo. of meeting between Hughes and Ambassador Geddes, 23 May 1921 (Library of Congress, C. E. Hughes MSS, box 175), Macardle, *Ir. republic*, p. 435n.

[93] Dumont to secretary of state, 28 Sept. 1920 (State Dept., 841d. 00/243).

[94] Ibid., 2 Jan. 1920 (State Dept., 841d.00/119).

[95] Ibid., 9 June 1921 (State Dept., 841d.00/381).

[96] First report of the cabinet committee on the Irish question, 4 Nov. 1919 cabinet paper 56 (CAB. 24/92).

would choose union with Britain,[97] but the need to satisfy opinion, particularly in the United States, demanded that Ulster should have a parliament, and indeed it was opened by King George V on 22 June, 1921. This was useful to the Anglo-Irish negotiations, which culminated in the treaty in December, in that it enabled unionists to accept the virtual independence granted to the Irish Free State, for Ulster no longer needed constitutional protection and was assured of partition, and it enabled Lloyd George to present a *fait accompli* to the nationalists which they had little choice but to accept.

Almost every Irish-American accepted the treaty of December 1921. They had never been very conscious of the differences between the notions of home rule, dominion status, self-government, national independence, partition, and so on. They were completely baffled by the civil war which broke out in the south in 1922 for, as far as they were concerned, the Irish were free, or at least sufficiently free to destroy the dynamic drive of the American movement. The new chaos in Ireland did not alter the fact that the Irish problem ceased to be an important factor in Anglo-American relations in December 1921. For too many years Britain had had to tolerate Irish interference in its relations with the United States because the Irish question, the cause of the trouble, was insoluble in the context of Anglo-Irish politics. The Irish still had an Irish problem, as the civil war made only too plain, and the British, faced with nationalist claims to Northern Ireland, still had an Irish problem, but there was no longer an American problem of Ireland of any great magnitude. Some of the hard-core Irish-American anglophobes did immerse themselves in the general wave of American isolationism, but they could never again collectively exercise a powerful influence as an Irish movement in its own right.

ALAN J. WARD

[97] Balfour memo. on Ireland, 25 Nov. 1919, cabinet paper 193 (CAB. 24/193).

THE IRISH-AMERICANS

An Arno Press Collection

Athearn, Robert G. **THOMAS FRANCIS MEAGHER:** An Irish Revolutionary in America. 1949

Biever, Bruce Francis. **RELIGION, CULTURE AND VALUES:** A Cross-Cultural Analysis of Motivational Factors in Native Irish and American Irish Catholicism. 1976

Bolger, Stephen Garrett. **THE IRISH CHARACTER IN AMERICAN FICTION, 1830-1860.** 1976

Browne, Henry J. **THE CATHOLIC CHURCH AND THE KNIGHTS OF LABOR.** 1949

Buckley, John Patrick. **THE NEW YORK IRISH:** Their View of American Foreign Policy, 1914-1921. 1976

Cochran, Alice Lida. **THE SAGA OF AN IRISH IMMIGRANT FAMILY:** The Descendants of John Mullanphy. 1976

Corbett, James J. **THE ROAR OF THE CROWD.** 1925

Cronin, Harry C. **EUGENE O'NEILL:** Irish and American; A Study in Cultural Context. 1976

Cuddy, Joseph Edward. **IRISH-AMERICAN AND NATIONAL ISOLATIONISM, 1914-1920.** 1976

Curley, James Michael. **I'D DO IT AGAIN:** A Record of All My Uproarious Years. 1957

Deasy, Mary. **THE HOUR OF SPRING.** 1948

Dinneen, Joseph. **WARD EIGHT.** 1936

Doyle, David Noel. **IRISH-AMERICANS, NATIVE RIGHTS AND NATIONAL EMPIRES:** The Structure, Divisions and Attitudes of the Catholic Minority in the Decade of Expansion, 1890-1901. 1976

Dunphy, Jack. **JOHN FURY.** 1946

Fanning, Charles, ed. **MR. DOOLEY AND THE CHICAGO IRISH:** An Anthology. 1976

Farrell, James T. **FATHER AND SON.** 1940

Fleming, Thomas J. **ALL GOOD MEN.** 1961

Funchion, Michael F. **CHICAGO'S IRISH NATIONALISTS, 1881-1890.** 1976

Gudelunas, William A., Jr. and William G. Shade. **BEFORE THE MOLLY MAGUIRES:** The Emergence of the Ethno-Religious Factor in the Politics of the Lower Anthracite Region, 1844-1872. 1976

Henderson, Thomas McLean. **TAMMANY HALL AND THE NEW IMMIGRANTS:** The Progressive Years. 1976

Hueston, Robert Francis. **THE CATHOLIC PRESS AND NATIVISM, 1840-1860.** 1976

Joyce, William Leonard. **EDITORS AND ETHNICITY:** A History of the Irish-American Press, 1848-1883. 1976

Larkin, Emmet. **THE HISTORICAL DIMENSIONS OF IRISH CATHOLICISM.** 1976

Lockhart, Audrey. **SOME ASPECTS OF EMIGRATION FROM IRELAND TO THE NORTH AMERICAN COLONIES BETWEEN 1660-1775.** 1976

Maguire, Edward J., ed. **REVEREND JOHN O'HANLON'S** *THE IRISH EMIGRANT'S GUIDE FOR THE UNITED STATES:* A Critical Edition with Introduction and Commentary. 1976

McCaffrey, Lawrence J., ed. **IRISH NATIONALISM AND THE AMERICAN CONTRIBUTION.** 1976

McDonald, Grace. **HISTORY OF THE IRISH IN WISCONSIN IN THE NINETEENTH CENTURY.** 1954

McManamin, Francis G. **THE AMERICAN YEARS OF JOHN BOYLE O'REILLY, 1870-1890.** 1976

McSorley, Edward. **OUR OWN KIND.** 1946

Moynihan, James H. **THE LIFE OF ARCHBISHOP JOHN IRELAND.** 1953

Niehaus, Earl F. **THE IRISH IN NEW ORLEANS, 1800-1860.** 1965

O'Grady, Joseph Patrick. **IRISH-AMERICANS AND ANGLO-AMERICAN RELATIONS, 1880-1888.** 1976

Rodechko, James Paul. **PATRICK FORD AND HIS SEARCH FOR AMERICA:** A Case Study of Irish-American Journalism, 1870-1913. 1976

Roney, Frank. **IRISH REBEL AND CALIFORNIA LABOR LEADER:** An Autobiography. Edited by Ira B. Cross. 1931

Roohan, James Edmund. **AMERICAN CATHOLICS AND THE SOCIAL QUESTION, 1865-1900.** 1976

Shannon, James. **CATHOLIC COLONIZATION ON THE WESTERN FRONTIER.** 1957

Shaw, Douglas V. **THE MAKING OF AN IMMIGRANT CITY:** Ethnic and Cultural Conflict in Jersey City, New Jersey, 1850-1877. 1976

Sylvester, Harry. **MOON GAFFNEY.** 1947

Tarpey, Marie Veronica. **THE ROLE OF JOSEPH McGARRITY IN THE STRUGGLE FOR IRISH INDEPENDENCE.** 1976

Vinyard, JoEllen McNergney. **THE IRISH ON THE URBAN FRONTIER:** Nineteenth Century Detroit. 1976

Walsh, James P., ed. **THE IRISH: AMERICA'S POLITICAL CLASS.** 1976

Weisz, Howard Ralph. **IRISH-AMERICAN AND ITALIAN-AMERICAN EDUCATIONAL VIEWS AND ACTIVITIES, 1870-1900:** A Comparison. 1976